# Agatha Christie
## TRIVIA

by
Richard T. Ryan

BELL PUBLISHING COMPANY
New York

This 1990 edition is published by Bell Publishing Company,
distributed by Crown Publishers, Inc.,
225 Park Avenue South,
New York, New York 10003,
by arrangement with Quinlan Press. Original edition published by
Quinlan Press in 1987.

Manufactured in the United States of America

Library of Congress Cataloging-in-Publication Data

Ryan, Richard T.
    Agatha Christie trivia / by Richard T. Ryan.
        p.     cm.
    ISBN 0-517-69917-6 (Crown)
    1. Christie, Agatha, 1890-1975—Miscellanea.   2. Detective and
mystery stories, English—Miscellanea.   3. Detective and mystery
films—Miscellanea.   4. Questions and answers.   I. Title.
    [Pr6005.H66Z84    1990]
    823′.912—dc20                                                           89-18165
                                                                                      CIP

h g f e d c b a

# DEDICATION

This book is dedicated to my wife, Grace, who not only does the impossible but quite often puts up with it as well.

# ACKNOWLEDGEMENTS

While writing this book was almost a labor of love for me, given my fondness for mysteries, there are a number of people who made my task so much easier than it would have been without their help. I am deeply indebted to both Joyce Kennedy and Judy Brennan for letting me borrow their copies of a number of hard-to-get-a-hold-of Christie novels. I am also thankful to Jeanne Logan, Cathy Imp, Rich Potter, Bob Edelman and Maureen Franz for their help in compiling and gathering the various materials needed for this book.

If I did not acknowledge the aid given by Gloria Gallo of London Weekend Television, Julie Quattro of HBO, and Joyce Wagner of Cannon Films, I should be terribly remiss.

I should be equally at fault if I failed to mention the help given by my mother, my sister, Arlene; and my very good friends Ed Burke and Lou Wein.

Finally, I need to acknowledge my editor, Sandy Bielawa, who is everything a writer could ask for in an editor — and more.

*Richard T. Ryan*
September 22, 1987

# Contents

# Titular Trivialitease

# Titular Trivialitease

1.  Agatha Christie's reputation rests on her achievements as a mystery writer, but how many of her novels and short story collections actually contain the word *mystery* or some form of it in their titles?

2.  If you're going to have a mystery, you have to give your readers clues as well. Can you come up with the only Christie title that actually contains the word *clue?*

3.  While a great many Christie stories have used two titles, how many of them have been graced with three, and how many of those titles can you recollect?

4.  One of Agatha Christie's best-loved creations was mystery writer Ariadne Oliver, who occa-

sionally dabbled as a detective. However, in one instance, Dame Agatha attributed a book to Ariadne with a title to which she must have been partial, for she later used it herself. Name the mystery that started out as one of Ariadne's and ended up as one of Agatha's.

5.   Though a number of Christie stories are set in the Middle East, only three titles contain references to places in that section of the world. What locations are mentioned by name?

6.   Everyone knows that Hercule Poirot once took part in an investigation into a *Murder on the Orient Express*. How many other trains figure in the titles of the Christie canon?

7.   Agatha Christie's favorite detective was the inimitable Poirot. Given that fact, in how many of her eighty-four mystery titles does the little Belgian's name appear?

8.   Though a prolific writer, Christie could occasionally become terse. Can you name the only two Christie titles that are single words?

9.   In that same vein, how many Christie titles are minor mysteries in themselves, in that they ask a question?

10.   *Dumb Witness* also has been released under the title *Poirot Loses a Client*. What was the name of the client?

11. Despite the colorful characters she created, Dame Agatha was apparently loath to use colors in her titles, as they appear in the names of only three of her works. How many of those vivid titles can you name?

12. Excluding the adjective *double*, numbers figure in twelve novel and short story collection titles by Christie. How many numerical *noms* can you recall?

13. What two holidays might we find in a perusal of the various novel and short story collection titles that make up the Christie canon?

14. Though she made use of a multitude of toxic agents in her novels and short stories, Dame Agatha mentions only one poison in her many titles. Can you remember that toxic title?

15. Quotations from a variety of literary sources figure prominently in a number of Christie titles. However, great authors notwithstanding, how many of her full-length mysteries have titles taken from nursery rhymes?

16. Portions of nursery rhymes also comprise the titles of two Poirot short stories. What are the names of those shorter efforts?

17. Animals also figure prominently in a number of titles. How many canines did Christie capitalize on in composing her titles?

5

18.     Which of the Christie titles is a direct quotation of a line from Shakespeare's *Macbeth*?

19.     Since murder seems to be a factor in many of the Bard's tragedies, it seems only fitting that one of Dame Agatha's many mysteries derives its title from a line in *Julius Caesar*. What is this oft-quoted title?

20.     Which Christie sleuth was actually consulted with regard to *The Regatta Mystery*?

21.     In a radical departure from her usual settings, Dame Agatha set one of her mysteries in Egypt in the year 2000 B.C. What is the title of that timeless tragedy?

22.     What is the name of the estate on which a *Murder After Hours* occurs? Incidentally, the name was also the British title of the book, and it comes from a poem by Tennyson.

23.     Can you recall the name of the character who was "coerced" into appearing as a "Witness for the Prosecution"?

24.     What is the actual name of the Leonides estate which looked at fancifully provides us with the inspiration for the title *Crooked House*?

25.     What was the name of Edward Sweetenham's play in *A Murder Is Announced* which with slight alterations later became one of Christie's own titles?

26. In which Christie mystery might we have involved ourselves had we been present at Little Paddocks at 6:30 p.m. on Friday, October 29?

27. What is the real name of the title character in "The Adventure of the Clapham Cook," which appears in *The Under Dog and Other Stories* — and which Christie sleuth is consulted in the matter?

28. What was the name of the character who was found murdered with "a pocket full of rye," thus giving the book its name?

29. Speaking of title characters, how many names used by *The Man in the Brown Suit* can you recall?

30. *What Mrs. McGillicuddy Saw!* was the original British title of *4:50 from Paddington*. However, even that title is a bit misleading. According to the novel, what time did the train actually depart?

31. As we mentioned earlier, animals figure in a great many Christie titles. Still, only a single volume contains the names of two different beasts in its title. Can you name it?

32. Although various sports are mentioned in almost every Christie mystery, only one novel's title actually contains a reference to a particular athletic endeavor. What was that sporting title?

33. As we mentioned earlier, Christie culled her titles from a wide variety of literary sources. Can you come up with the only title that can be found in the Bible?

34. One of Christie's more delightful mysteries was *The Clocks.* Can you remember exactly how many timepieces were introduced into Miss Millicent Pebmarsh's sitting room, and at what time they had been set?

35. What is the only Christie title that refers to a location on the American side of the Atlantic?

36. We all know that Norma Restarick was the *Third Girl.* In their proper order give the names of the first and second girls.

37. Which of Dame Agatha's titles may be found in a poem by William Blake?

38. In all of her many titles, short stories included, Christie uses the names of only two days of the week. What are these timely titles?

39. Specifically, what holiday do we find being "celebrated" in *A Holiday for Murder*?

40. Which Christie title is taken from the poem "Gates of Damascus," by John Flecker, whom she also quoted in *Parker Pyne Investigates*?

41. *Sleeping Murder,* though released as her last book, was written during World War II.

Although it is Miss Jane Marple's swan song, one of its chapters has the same name as a Poirot mystery composed during the same period. Can you call to mind this common title?

42. *Sleeping Murder* may have been the last Christie mystery to be released, but what was actually the last book that she wrote?

43. While working on *A Caribbean Mystery*, Miss Marple refers to herself by the title of another novel in which she appears. What word, of Hellenic origin, did Miss Marple use to describe herself?

44. Speaking of twice-told tales, can you name the title shared by a Parker Pyne short story and a Hercule Poirot novel?

45. Finally: Most of Dame Agatha's mysteries involve the crime of murder. How many different titles in the Christie canon contain the word *murder?* Count only full-length works.

# Answers

1.  She used the word *mystery* in seven titles —
    only one of which, *A Caribbean Mystery*, was
    written after 1934.

2.  *The Boomerang Clue*, which is also titled
    *Why Didn't They Ask Evans?*

3.  Appropriately enough, three Christie mys-
    teries have appeared under three different
    titles. They are: 1) *Hercule Poirot's Christmas
    / Murder for Christmas / A Holiday for Mur-
    der;* 2) *Ten Little Niggers / And Then There
    Were None / Ten Little Indians;* 3) *One, Two,
    Buckle My Shoe / The Patriotic Murders /
    An Overdose of Death.*

4.  *The Body in the Library*

5.  Mesopotamia, the Nile and Baghdad

6.  Three: *The Blue Train,* the *4:50 from Paddington* and "The Plymouth Express"

7.  Surprisingly enough, Poirot's name appears in only four titles.

8.  That "singular" distinction belongs to *Nemesis* and *Curtain.*

9.  Two: *Why Didn't They Ask Evans?* And *N or M?*

10. Emily Arundell

11. *The Man in the Brown Suit, The Mystery of the Blue Train* and *The Golden Ball and Other Stories*

12. *The Big Four, Seven Dials, 13 Problems, 13 at Dinner, Murder in Three Acts, Ten Little Indians, One, Two, Buckle My Shoe, Five Little Pigs, Towards Zero, Three Blind Mice, 4:50 from Paddington* and *Third Girl*

13. Christmas and Hallowe'en

14. *Sparkling Cyanide*

15. Eight: *Ten Little Indians, One Two, Buckle My Shoe, Five Little Pigs, Three Blind Mice, A Pocket Full of Rye, Hickory Dickory Death, Crooked House* and *Mrs. McGinty's Dead*

16. "Four and Twenty Blackbirds" and "How Does Your Garden Grow?"

17. Two: *The Hound of Death* and *The Under Dog*

18. *By the Pricking of My Thumbs*

19. *There Is a Tide*

20. Parker Pyne

21. *Death Comes As the End*

22. *The Hollow*

23. Romaine Heilger

24. Three Gables

25. Sweetenham wrote *Elephants Do Forget*, which Dame Agatha later altered to *Elephants Can Remember.*

26. *A Murder Is Announced*

27. Eliza Dunn was "The Clapham Cook," and Poirot was retained to locate her.

28. Rex Fortescue

29. At different times he was known as Harry Rayburn, Harry Parker, Harry Lucas and John Harold Eardsley.

30. 4:54

31. *Cat Among the Pigeons*

32. *Murder on the Links*

33. *The Pale Horse*

34. Four clocks set at 4:13

35. *A Caribbean Mystery*

36. Claudia Reece-Holland was the "first girl" and Frances Cary was the second.

37. *Endless Night*

38. *The Tuesday Club Murders* and "Fruitful Sunday"

39. Christmas

40. *Postern of Fate*

41. Chapter 5 of *Sleeping Murder* is titled "Murder in Retrospect".

42. *Postern of Fate*

43. Miss Maple calls herself "Nemesis."

44. *Death on the Nile*

45. The word *murder* may be found in eighteen different titles.

# A Poirot Perspective

# A Poirot Perspective

1.      Prior to *The Mysterious Affair at Styles*, Poirot
        had worked with Detective Inspector Japp in
        1904. Can you recall the name of the case
        in which those two first joined forces?

2.      What was the name of the estate that Poirot
        shared with a number of other Belgian
        refugees in *The Mysterious Affair at Styles*?

3.      Soon after, Poirot moved to London, where
        he shared rooms with Hastings. What was
        Poirot's address during the period that he was
        rooming with his chronicler?

4.      What two words does Hastings tell us are
        Poirot's "gods"?

5.      Hastings constantly refers to Poirot's rather sizeable watch by comparing it to a vegetable—a rather unusual analogy but apparently an apt one. What type of vegetable is Poirot's timepiece said to resemble?

6.      In his first attempt at retirement in England, the little Belgian moved to the country. What was the name of Poirot's house in *The Murder of Roger Ackroyd*?

7.      Abandoning retirement, Poirot once again returned to London. What was his last address in that city, a residence chosen for its "strictly geometrical appearance and proportions"?

8.      What was the number of Poirot's flat at that address?

9.      Hercule Poirot had two phone numbers while he was living in London. Can you remember either of them?

10.     In a second attempt at life in the country, Poirot rented a country estate. What was the name of the house leased by Poirot shortly before he became involved with a *Murder After Hours*?

11.     How tall is the little Belgian?

12.     What color are Poirot's eyes?

13. What unusual activity does Poirot engage in "to soothe his nerves" when he is upset?

14. An inveterate smoker, what type of cigarettes does Poirot prefer?

15. We all know that Poirot is so vain that he colors his hair. What is the name of the dye he favors?

16. In addition to his other qualities, Poirot is an epicure at heart. Without a doubt, what is the favorite meal of the day of this gourmet detective?

17. Poirot, when he opts for an alcoholic beverage, usually chooses a sweet liquor. What is his personal favorite?

18. Still, all things considered, something else would have to be considered Poirot's favorite beverage, bedtime or otherwise. What is it?

19. What religion does Poirot practice?

20. Thrifty by nature, Poirot seldom speculates; however, he does own stock. Can you name the only company in which Poirot is a shareholder?

21. What was the alias employed by Poirot when he pretended to be writing a biography of General Arundell in *Poirot Loses a Client*?

22. Like most great detectives, Hercule Poirot evidenced literary aspirations. What exactly was the subject of his *magnum opus*?

23. Almost as distinctive as his moustaches is Poirot's footwear. What type of shoes does our well-shod sleuth don regularly?

24. Poirot hates the sea almost as much as he despises disorder. Still, there are times when travel is unavoidable. Whose method does Poirot employ to cure his *mal de mer* when he journeys abroad?

25. Although Poirot did not often use aliases, in "The Third Floor Flat" he assumed what would seem to be an incongruous one. What was the little Belgian's *nom de guerre* in that particular case?

26. Poirot once told Hastings, "All celebrated detectives have brothers who would be even more celebrated than they, were it not for constitutional indolence." What is the name of Poirot's "twin brother," who lives "near Spa in Belgium"?

27. What is the only case in which he appears?

28. On more than one occasion Poirot's love of symmetry proved invaluable. In which case did Poirot's passion for order and neatness — in this instance manifested by straightening items on a mantle — help him to land a murderer by the heels?

29. Despite his love of order, the case was always paramount to Poirot. What was the name of the disorganized, unmethodical guest house that Poirot endured while working on the case of Mrs. McGinty's murder?

30. After Hastings's marriage and departure, Poirot hired a valet. What is the name of Poirot's impassive, thoroughly English, gentleman's gentleman?

31. What is the name of the Scotland Yard inspector with whom Poirot most frequently worked?

32. Another long-time friend was a Russian noblewoman. Can you name the first case in which that Hercule Poirot met the Countess Vera Rossakoff, a woman whom he remained fond of for the rest of his life?

33. Poirot was not above taking the law into his own hands upon occasion. In "The Veiled Lady" he burgled a home in hopes of helping a client. Who hired Poirot, and whose home did he rob?

34. In another instance Poirot, needing proof, manufactured "evidence" and used "a small square of green chiffon" to help him arrive at the truth. In which case did Poirot prevaricate to arrive at the truth?

35. Had he been captured in the act described above, Poirot might have needed an attorney. What is the name of Poirot's solicitors?

36.  In *Peril at End House,* Poirot admits to failing once — "in Belgium in 1893." He claimed that it was an affair involving what rather pedestrian object?

37.  Poirot numbered another full-length case among his few failures because he never would have solved it but for "the chance remark of a stranger." Which case did he refuse to add to his innumerable triumphs?

38.  Can you recall the case that compelled Poirot to return to England, and thus was at least indirectly responsible for his involvement with a *Murder on the Orient Express?*

39.  On the train Poirot was shuffled around a bit. What was the number of his final compartment on the Orient Express?

40.  Poirot usually sought the limelight, but not always. Can you name the case in which Poirot willingly played a supporting role so as to advance a romance?

41.  It may seem amazing, but Poirot was once almost indicted for murder. In which of his many adventures was he nearly arrested for the murder of one of his traveling companions?

42.  Exactly how many "labors" did the little Belgian set for himself in seeking to reprise the well-known feats of his classical namesake?

43. In *Death in the Air* Poirot temporarily hired a young woman as his secretary. What was her name?

44. The above-mentioned woman was soon replaced by an unusually reliable woman. What is the name of Poirot's rather unimaginative confidential secretary, who never thinks unless told to do so?

45. In which case did Poirot, who was not especially fond of the outdoors, plan a picnic on Dartmoor to see if someone had told him a "little lie"?

46. In one case a woman came to Poirot claiming that the initials "H. P." had been repeated several times on her Ouija board. What case had this rather otherwordly beginning?

47. What was the only case in which Poirot, who normally did "not approve of murder," condoned one by accepting an "official" verdict which he knew to be erroneous?

48. What was the name of Poirot's valet in *Curtain,* his final case?

49. The pride of Poirot's life were his luxurious moustaches. In which two cases might the observant onlooker have seen Poirot sporting an artificial adornment on his upper lip?

50. Finally, what words did Poirot instruct Hastings to whisper if he should "think at any time" that Poirot was "growing conceited"?

# Answers

1. They had collaborated on the Abercrombie forgery case.

2. Leastways Cottage

3. 14 Farraway Street

4. As we all know, Poirot worships "Order and Method."

5. A turnip

6. The Larches

7. Whitehaven Mansions

8. Poirot occupied flat number 203.

9. Poirot could be reached at Trafalgar 8137 and at Whitehall 7272.

10. Poirot leased the inappropriately named Resthaven.

11. "Hardly more than 5 foot 4"

12. Green

13. He builds card houses.

14. He smokes "little Russian cigarettes."

15. Revivit

16. Poirot lives for *le diner!*

17. *Sirop de cassis*

18. Hot chocolate

19. He is a practicing Roman Catholic.

20. He has fourteen thousand shares in Burma Mines, Ltd.

21. In an unusual display of pedestrian thinking, Poirot called himseld "Parotti."

22. Poirot authored a book on great writers of detective fiction.

23. Tight, pointed, patent leather shoes

24. Poirot uses the method of Laverguier to avoid seasickness.

25. Looking nothing like an Irishman, Poirot nevertheless rented the flat under the name of O'Connor.

26. Achille

27. *The Big Four* marks the only appearance of Achille in the Christie canon.

28. *The Mysterious Affair at Styles*

29. Long Meadows, located in Broadhinny

30. George(s)

31. Inspector James "Jimmy" Japp

32. They first encountered each other in "The Double Clue," in *Double Sin*.

33. Poirot burgled the home of Mr. Lavington at the request of Lady Millicent Castle Vaughn.

34. "The Under Dog"

35. Poirot retains the firm of McNeill and Hodgson.

36. A box of chocolates

37. *13 at Dinner*

38. The Kassner Case

39. Poirot was finally installed in compartment number 1.

40. *Murder in Three Acts*

41. It sounds impossible, but, *tout de meme,* it almost happened in *Death in the Air.*

42. Twelve

43. Jane Grey

44. Miss Lemon

45. *Evil Under the Sun*

46. *There Is a Tide*

47. *Murder on the Orient Express*

48. Curtiss

49. *The Big Four* and *Curtain* saw Poirot *sans* his true moustaches.

50. Hastings was told to whisper "chocolate box" should Poirot ever grow conceited, but such a thing — *c'est impossible!*

# Mon Ami Hastings

# *Mon Ami* Hastings

1. Despite the fact that he started out as Poirot's Watson, Hastings does not appear in all that many cases. In how many novels does Hastings appear with Poirot?

2. In *The Mysterious Affair at Styles,* what did Hastings say he had done "before the war"?

3. At the outbreak of the war, Hastings joined the army and was subsequently wounded. During what battle did Poirot's biographer sustain an injury which resulted in his being discharged from the army?

4. What was Hastings's rank when he was discharged from the service?

5.    Who was Hastings's childhood friend who invited him to Styles and thus was indirectly responsible for his reunion with Poirot?

6.    On what date were Hastings and Poirot reunited, after a separation of some years, and thus able to join forces to unravel *The Mysterious Affair at Styles?*

7.    Much younger than Poirot, how old was Hastings — within two years — at the time of *The Mysterious Affair at Styles?*

8.    While staying at Styles, Hastings imagined himself in love with two different women and actually proposed to one of them. Can you remember the objects of Hastings's misplaced *amor?*

9.    The romantic impulses of Hastings may be ascribed in part to his preference for women with a particular hair color. What shade of hair is the good Hastings often, and truly, accused of being partial to?

10.   How was Hastings employed when he and Poirot were asked to solve the *Murder on the Links?*

11.   In what year did Hastings meet his wife? Hint: It was the same year Poirot solved the *Murder on the Links.*

12.   In that same case Hastings met the woman he would wed on a train. What fairy-tale name did the future Mrs. Hastings give as her own?

13. If you remembered that, then surely you can remember her real name?

14. What was the first name of Hastings's sister-in-law, as well as the stage name of the delightful Duveen twins?

15. In what theater did Hastings see his wife perform?

16. To which South American country did Hastings move after he had left Poirot and married?

17. What are the nicknames by which Hastings refers to his wife?

18. Thus far, we have referred to Hastings only by his surname. What is the Christian name of *mon ami* Hastings?

19. What was the first full-length case in which Hastings became involved after his marriage and move to South America?

20. Poirot was once given a dog, which he in turn relinquished to his companion. What was the name of Hastings's canine companion, and what kind of dog was it?

21. During *The Big Four* Hastings went undercover and served as secretary to one of the gang's leaders. What was the alias he assumed?

22. In one short story Hastings, acting as Poirot's agent while the little Belgian was down with the flu, did all the legwork. In which adventure did Hastings distinguish himself under Poirot's direction?

23. Can you recall the type of moustache preferred by Hastings and hated by Poirot?

24. Although Hastings did not possess the gray cells "of the quality" of Poirot's, he could think quickly enough in a tight situation. What two items did Hastings leave in groups of four to tip off Poirot in *The Big Four*?

25. Believe it or not, Hastings once seriously considered murdering someone. In which case did it occur, and what was the name of the prospective victim?

26. How many children did Hastings have, and can you name the only one who figures in a Christie novel?

27. In addition to the child mentioned in the question above, we know the name of one other of Hastings's progeny. What is it?

28. What is the name of Hastings's son-in-law, and what is his profession?

29. What were the last instructions that Hastings ever received from Poirot?

30. What were the last words spoken to Hastings by his *bon ami*, Poirot, in *Curtain*?

# Answers

1. Hastings is present in only eight novels.

2. Hastings had been employed by Lloyds of London.

3. The Somme

4. Captain

5. John Cavendish

6. That fateful meeting occurred on Monday, July 16, 1916.

7. He was approximately thirty years old.

8.     Hastings believed himself in love with Mary Cavendish and Cynthia Murdoch; he proposed to Miss Murdoch.

9.     Hastings has always had a fondness for auburn hair.

10.    As a secretary to a Member of Parliament

11.    1921

12.    The future Mrs. Hastings called herself Cinderella.

13.    Dulcie Duveen

14.    Dulcie and Bella Duveen billed themselves, appropriately enough, as "The Dulcibella Kids."

15.    The Palace in Coventry

16.    Argentina

17.    He continued to call her Cinderella, and later, "Cinders."

18.    Arthur

19.    *The Big Four*

20.    Bob was a wire-haired terrier.

21.    Hastings's *nom de guerre* on that occasion was Major Arthur Neville.

22. Hastings outdid himself solving "The Mystery of Hunter's Lodge."

23. Hastings sported a "toothbrush" moustache — an object of scorn for Poirot.

24. Hastings left books and coals as tips for Poirot.

25. In *Curtain* Hastings planned to do away with Major Allerton.

26. Hastings had four children; his daughter Judith was a principal character in *Curtain*, Poirot's last case.

27. Grace

28. Dr. John Franklin is a specialist in the research of tropical diseases.

29. In a note received after Poirot's death, Hastings was instructed to "Talk to my valet, Georges."

30. The last words Hastings heard Poirot speak were "*Cher ami.*"

# Jane and Ariadne, Distaff Detectives

# Jane & Ariadne, Distaff Detectives

1. In what country was Miss Jane Marple educated, and can you also come up with the city in which she attended school?

2. Miss Marple lives in a small village, but because human nature is the same everywhere, she simply draws parallels between events in her village and those that occur elsewhere. What is the name of Miss Marple's microcosm?

3. Everyone knows that Miss Marple is extraordinarily observant. What color are the dear lady's eyes, with which she "sees everything"?

4. In *Murder at the Vicarage,* her first case, what does Miss Marple tell us her hobby is?

5. One way to keep abreast of human nature is to keep up with the news. How many newspapers does Miss Marple get each day?

6. Who is Miss Marple's closest friend in her village?

7. In which type of house does Jane Marple live: Queen Anne, Georgian or Victorian?

8. When Miss Marple needs to take a taxi, whom does she ask her maid to call?

9. What is Miss Marple's phone number?

10. Once she began taking an interest in murder, Miss Marple became friendly with the local constabulary. Who is the chief constable for Radfordshire, which includes Miss Marple's village?

11. One of the great constants and comforts in Miss Marple's life is her nephew. What is his name, and what does he do for a living?

12. If you remembered the answer to the above question, then you should have little difficulty recalling the maiden name of Miss Marple's nephew's wife, since both she and her husband-to-be were charter members of the Tuesday Night Club.

13. What is the name of Miss Marple's solicitor? If it's any help, he also happened to be a charter member of the Tuesday Night Club.

14. Though Miss Marple was the first to arrive at the correct solution in *A Murder Is Announced*, she had some help from a member of the official force, who just happened to be Sir Henry Clithering's godson. What was the young man's name?

15. Miss Marple's next-door neighbor was her physician as well as the police surgeon for the village. Can you recall the name of this doctor, who rendered Miss Marple invaluable assistance on more than one occasion?

16. Throughout her life, Miss Marple employed a goodly number of servants. What was the name of her honest but easily flustered maid at the time of "The Case of the Perfect Maid"?

17. Miss Marple's nephew hired a live-in companion for his aunt in her later years. Unfortunately, they were less than compatible. What was the name of that vivacious virago?

18. Whom did Miss Marple choose as the successor to the answer to the above question?

19. Speaking of servants, what was the name of the faithful former maid with whom Miss Marple resided while she was trying to determine exactly *What Mrs. McGillicuddy Saw*?

20. What was the name of the vicar's wife in *The Moving Finger* who asked Jane Marple to investigate the poison pen letters that were plaguing her village?

21.     In that same vein, name the village that was suffering that particular form of persecution.

22.     In *A Pocket Full of Rye* a girl that Miss Marple had "trained for service" was murdered and a clothespin stuck on her nose. Miss Marple was incensed at the treatment the dead girl had received and felt obliged to avenge her death. What was the name of the young girl whose death so aroused Miss Marple?

23.     Because of her age Miss Marple was unable to do the necessary legwork to find out *What Mrs. McGillicuddy Saw,* so she hired someone to help her. What was the name of the person Miss Marple employed to find the body of an unknown dead woman?

24.     Though she often traveled within England, Miss Marple seldom left it. However, on one noteworthy occasion she enjoyed a vacation in the Caribbean. Can you remember both the hotel and the island where Miss Marple stayed while investigating *A Caribbean Mystery?*

25.     With whom did Miss Marple join forces to solve *A Caribbean Mystery* and prevent yet another tragedy?

26.     Miss Marple was truly a gifted amateur detective, yet once she was offered remuneration for her services. What was the only case in which Miss Marple was paid for her avocation of sleuthing, and who put up the money to pay her?

27. Which of Miss Marple's many cases had an almost choric-like refrain running throughout it in the form of the maxim: "No smoke without fire"?

28. What was the name of the village in which Miss Marple wrapped up *Sleeping Murder*, her last case?

29. *Sleeping Murder* was the last Jane Marple mystery published. Do you know which was the last one written?

30. In *Nemesis* Miss Marple took a bus tour. What was the number of the tour that had been booked for Miss Marple?

31. Ariadne Oliver was once employed by Parker Pyne. Can you name either of the cases in which she aided and abetted his efforts?

32. What was the first full-length case on which Mrs. Oliver collaborated — if we can use that term — with Hercule Poirot?

33. In her long literary career Ariadne Oliver turned out a great many best-sellers. Within ten, how many books does Dame Agatha credit her with composing?

34. Like her creator, Ariadne Oliver created a celebrated detective from a foreign country. What nationality was her sleuth, and what was his name?

35.     Although she wrote fictional mysteries, Mrs. Oliver often worked with Poirot solving real-life murders. Exactly how many cases did she and Poirot share, and how many of them can you name?

36.     Aside from her well-known partiality to apples, Mrs. Oliver has one other obvious trait. With what aspect of her appearance is Mrs. Oliver constantly experimenting?

37.     In which London typing service might we see a picture of Ariadne Oliver adorning the office walls of the proprietress, Miss Martindale?

38.     What was the name of Ariadne Oliver's nanny who turned out to be a prize pachyderm in *Elephants Can Remember*?

39.     What was the name of the young man who was adapting one of Ariadne's novels for the stage and with whom she was collaborating when she met Poirot, who was looking into the death of Mrs. McGinty?

40.     Obviously color was on her mind, for while she was working on the case of *The Pale Horse*, Ariadne Oliver was busy composing a novel of her own with a colorful title. Which one was it?

41.     With whom was Ariadne staying when she got involved with a murder at a *Hallowe'en Party*?

42. To which fruit did Ariadne become partial after her unpleasant experience with apples at the same *Hallowe'en Party?*

43. Can you recall the apt sobriquet Mrs. Oliver bestowed on David Baker in *Third Girl?*

44. In which book was Ariadne Oliver commissioned to devise a "Murder Hunt" which, much to her chagrin and sorrow, ended up with a real corpse instead of a pretend one?

45. What was the name of the young girl who was really murdered in Mrs. Oliver's staged "Murder Hunt"?

46. Normally Ariadne Oliver avoided publicity and shunned affairs such as literary luncheons; however, on one occasion she attended such a function and met a rather obnoxious woman who caused her to find out if *Elephants Can Remember.* What was that character's name?

47. One reason Mrs. Oliver became involved in that case was because the woman in the above question was the mother of the boy who wanted to marry her goddaughter. What is the name of Mrs. Oliver's goddaughter, who caused both Ariadne and Poirot to seek out metaphorical elephants?

48. In *Mrs. McGinty's Dead* Ariadne Oliver mentions the titles of three of her books. How many of these can you recall?

49.     Here's a real stumper. What was the title of
        the book by Mrs. Oliver that was inspired by
        her experiences at Nasse House in *Dead
        Man's Folly?*

50.     Finally, though she usually worked with Poirot,
        Mrs. Oliver appears in one novel without the
        little Belgian. In which book does Mrs. Oliver
        solo?

# Answers

1.  Miss Marple attended a *pensionnat* in Florence, Italy.

2.  St. Mary Mead

3.  Her eyes are often described as being "china blue."

4.  Human nature

5.  Two

6.  Dolly Bantry

7.  Georgian

8. She calls Inch's taxi — even though Inch hasn't owned it in a great many years. Old habits die hard.

9. 35

10. Colonel Melchett

11. Raymond West is a novelist who writes books about "unpleasant people."

12. Joyce Lempriere

13. Mr. Petherick handles Miss Marple's legal affairs.

14. Detective Inspector Dermot Craddock

15. Dr. Haydock

16. Miss Marple's maid at that time was named Edna.

17. Miss Knight

18. Cherry Baker and her husband, Jim

19. Florence

20. Mrs. Dane Calthrop

21. Lymstock

22. Gladys Martin

50

23. The name of that incredibly competent young lady was Lucy Eylesbarrow.

24. She vacationed at the Golden Palm Hotel on the island of St. Honore'

25. Mr. Jason Rafiel

26. In *Nemesis* she was paid by Mr. Rafiel, whom she had first encountered in the Caribbean.

27. *The Moving Finger*

28. She solved her last case in the village of Dillmouth.

29. The last Miss Marple mystery that Dame Agatha wrote was *Nemesis*.

30. Tour #37: "Famous Homes and Gardens"

31. Mrs. Oliver helped Mr. Pyne with "The Case of the Discontented Soldier" as well as "The Case of the Rich Woman."

32. Although they had met previously at a literary luncheon, Mrs. Oliver and Poirot first worked together in *Cards on the Table*.

33. Mrs. Oliver had ostensibly written forty-six best-sellers.

34. Mrs. Oliver's creation was Sven Hjerson, a Finn.

35. She and Poirot worked together six times: *Cards on the Table, Mrs. McGinty's Dead, Dead Man's Folly, Third Girl, Hallowe'en Party* and *Elephants Can Remember.*

36. She is forever trying out new hairdos.

37. The Cavendish Secretarial and Typing Bureau boasts Mrs. Oliver among their many well-known clients.

38. Mrs. Matcham

39. Robin Upwood

40. *The White Cockatoo*

41. She was staying with Judith Butler and her daughter Miranda.

42. She started to eat dates.

43. She referred to him as "the Peacock Boy" or simply as "the Peacock."

44. *Dead Man's Folly*

45. Marlene Tucker

46. Mrs. Burton-Cox

47. Celia Ravenscroft

48. She refers to *The Affair of the Second Goldfish, Death of a Debutante* and *The Cat It Was Who Died.*

49.     *The Woman in the Wood*

50.     She appears in *The Pale Horse* without Poirot.

# Tommy and Tuppence, "No Unreasonable Offer Refused"

# Tommy and Tuppence, "No Unreasonable Offer Refused"

1.  In their first adventure Tommy and Tuppence formed a "joint venture" and advertised in the *Times*. What was the name of their corporation?

2.  In that fateful ad they stated "no unreasonable offer refused." How many responses did they get to their initial ad, and how many of the respondents can you remember?

3.  What is Tuppence's real Christian name, and can you also come up with her middle initial?

4.  Where was Tuppence from, and what did her father do for a living?

5.    At the time of their first adventure Tommy had recently been demobilized from the British army. How many times had he been wounded in the war?

6.    Can you name the only relative of Tommy's, not counting his children, who appears in their adventures?

7.    In their first undertaking, tracking down *The Secret Adversary,* a ship figured prominently. What was the name of that ill-fated vessel?

8.    During the course of their investigations, they became involved with a Scotland Yard officer. What was the name of their first contact at the Yard?

9.    Unwittingly, Tommy and Tuppence blundered into something big in *The Secret Adversary* and as a result became involved with the British Secret Service. What was the name used by the agent who was their first contact with the Secret Service and who, in effect, hired Tommy and Tuppence as freelance operatives?

10.    Many years later Tommy and Tuppence learned that their contact was actually the head of the Secret Service, as well as a nobleman. What is the proper title of their intelligence-service contact?

11. *The Secret Adversary* centers around a missing girl whom Tommy and Tuppence were determined to locate. What was the name of that elusive young woman?

12. What was the code name used by *The Secret Adversary,* a man those in the know regarded as "the master criminal of this age"?

13. While tracking down *The Secret Adversary* Tommy and Tuppence encountered a young elevator boy. What is the name of that jack-of-all-trades who remained with them for the rest of their careers?

14. In *Partners in Crime* Tommy and Tuppence were set up in business. What was the name of the firm that the Beresfords managed?

15. What were the aliases used by Tommy and Tuppence for the majority of the cases in *Partners in Crime?*

16. Hank Ryder was an American from Alabama who was given a most distinctive nickname by Tommy — before they even met. What was the descriptive *nom?*

17. In a rather curious overlapping, it would seem that Tommy, Tuppence and Hercule Poirot were called into and solved the same case. Which of the adventures in *Partners in Crime* was apparently solved by both the Beresfords and Poirot?

18. In a wonderful self-parody, Dame Agatha has Tommy pretend to be Poirot during the final chapter of the *Partners* volume. What is the name of the engaging short story that offers us Tommy-Hercule, or two sleuths for the price of one?

19. By the time Tommy and Tuppence got involved in the *N or M?* adventure, they were a happily married couple with two children. What were the names of the younger Beresfords?

20. What is Tommy affectionately called by his offspring?

21. Later on Tommy and Tuppence adopted a child. Can you remember the name of, and in what case they first encountered, their future child?

22. In his later years the stalwart assistant of Tommy and Tuppence became a pub owner in South London. What was the name of his establishment?

23. How old was Tommy when World War II broke out and he was brought into the *N or M?* adventure?

24. By the time that particular case rolled around, the Beresfords' usual intelligence contact had retired. Who replaced him?

25. Since the *N or M?* adventure required under-cover work, both Tommy and Tuppence adopted aliases. What were the names they used while tracking down the German spies working in England?

26. As part of her undercover background, Tuppence pretended to have a number of sons in various branches of the service. How many children did she claim to have, and how many of their names can you remember?

27. Most of the pursuit of the mysterious M and N happened in the neighborhood of a guest house where Tommy and Tuppence were staying. Can you recall the name of the guest house at which Tommy, who was officially on the case, and Tuppence, who wasn't, stayed during the *N or M?* question?

28. In addition to using them for titles, Dame Agatha occasionally employed nursery rhymes as integral parts of her stories. Which children's favorite played a vital role in the very adult problems posed by *N or M?* ?

29. What was the name of Tommy's aunt in *By the Pricking of My Thumbs,* whose stay at Sunny Ridge was in large part responsible for their involvement in that case?

30. A picture of a house by a canal played an important role in that same case. What was the artist's name?

31. How many different names for the estate in that painting can you recall?

32. Near the end of his long career Tommy was working for the I.U.A.S. What do the initials stand for?

33. In *Postern of Fate* Tommy met the enigmatic Mr. Robinson. What code phrase did Robinson instruct Tommy to use if he came across anything important?

34. At the same time the local police official, Inspector Norris, and Tommy agreed upon the use of a Biblical code word to prevent imposters from infiltrating their organization. What was this word of wisdom?

35. Exactly how did "Oxford" and "Cambridge" figure in the outcome of *Postern of Fate,* Tommy and Tuppence's last case?

36. Another important figure in *Postern of Fate* was Tommy and Tuppence's Manchester terrier. Can you remember the name of their extremely protective canine?

37. When Tommy and Tuppence finally retired to the country, they bought a house. What was the name of their estate?

38. Near the end of *Postern of Fate* Tommy and Tuppence are visited by their grandchildren. How many of those potential detectives *extraordinaire* can you call to mind?

# Answers

1. They called themselves the "Young Adventurers Ltd."

2. They received two replies; one was from Julius P. Hersheimmer and the other from an A. Carter.

3. Tuppence was christened Prudence L. Cowley.

4. She was the fifth daughter of Archdeacon Cowley of Little Missendell, Suffolk.

5. Twice: once in France and once while serving in Mesopotamia

6. Tommy's only relative who appears in any of their stories is his uncle, Sir William Beresford.

7. The *Lusitania*

8. They worked with none other than Inspector James "Jimmy" Japp.

9. Mr. A. Carter

10. Mr. Carter was really Lord Easthampton.

11. Jane Finn

12. Mr. Brown

13. Albert Batt

14. Blunt's International Detective Agency

15. Tommy was Mr. Blunt while Tuppence pretended to be Miss Robinson, his secretary. However, Tuppence also used the names Ganges and Sheringham.

16. Tommy called him "The Crackler."

17. In *Partners in Crime* Tommy and Tuppence handled the case of "The Ambassador's Boots," while in *13 at Dinner* Poirot took some time out from the main investigation to handle the exact same case.

18. "The Man Who Was No. 16"

19. The Beresford twins were named Deborah and Derek.

20. Carrots or Carrot-top

21. They adopted a girl named Betty, whom they met in the *N or M?* affair.

22. Albert's pub was called The Duck and Dog.

23. Forty-six

24. Mr. Grant replaced Mr. Carter.

25. Tommy posed as Mr. Meadowes, while Tuppence passed herself off as Mrs. Blenkensop.

26. Mrs. Blenkensop claimed to have three sons named Douglas, Raymond and Cyril.

27. The guest house was named Sans Souci.

28. "Goosey, Goosey, Gander"

29. Ada Fanshaw

30. William Boscowan

31. At different times it was called Watermead, Waterside, Riverbank, Ladymead, Canal House, Bridge House, Canal Side, Meadowside and Riverside.

32. International Union of Associated Security

33. Mr. Robinson told Tommy to use the phrase "crab apple jelly."

34. Solomon

35.     Oxford and Cambridge were the names given
        to two garden stools because of their colors.
        One of the stools contained secret documents.

36.     Hannibal

37.     The Laurels was its name when they pur-
        chased it, although it had been called a great
        many other things, including Katmandu, by
        previous owners.

38.     Tommy and Tuppence's grandchildren are
        named Andrew, Janet and Rosalie.

# Secondary Sleuths

# Secondary Sleuths

1.    One of Christie's more popular creations was *The Mysterious Mr. Quin*. Like most great detectives, he never worked alone. Can you remember Mr. Quin's accomplice and aide in each of his adventures?

2.    An inn, appropriately named, figures in more than one of the mysterious Mr. Quin's cases. What is the colorful name of that country eatery?

3.    Can you recall either one of the artists who drew *The Mysterious Mr. Quin*? One sketched him, while the other painted him in oils.

4.    Mr. Harley Quin is a music lover, as well he should be. To which Verdi opera is he particularly partial?

5.	Another Christie creation was a retired gentleman turned detective and "heart specialist." What did the pleasant Parker Pyne do for a living before he retired to pursue his new careers?

6.	What is Parker Pyne's address?

7.	As far as we know, Parker Pyne is the only Christie protagonist who advertises his services. Where does Mr. Pyne place his advertisements?

8.	According to the philosophical Parker Pyne, how many "main headings of unhappiness" are there?

9.	What was the name of Mr. Pyne's confidential secretary?

10.	Secretaries aside, how many other members of Parker Pyne's incredibly varied staff can you name?

11.	In "The Oracle at Delphi" Parker Pyne, while traveling under an assumed name, heard his own name being used by a person pretending to be Pyne. What was Pyne's name in that tale, and who was the blackguard imposter?

12.	Although we know him primarily as Parker Pyne, what is Mr. Parker Pyne's true Christian name?

13. Although Superintendent Battle figures in five Christie mysteries, we know very little about him. However, we do know that he and his wife had a number of little Battles. Exactly how many children were there in the Battle household?

14. What is the name of the Battles's youngest child, whose experience at school provided the Superintendent with a Marple-like parallel which he used to clear a woman in *Towards Zero*?

15. Apparently police work must run in the Battle family. What is the name of the Superintendent's nephew who was originally assigned to investigate the murder of Lady Tressilian in *Towards Zero*?

16. We've already given you a couple of hints. How many of the five Superintendent Battle books can you name?

17. Battle and Colonel Johnny Race joined forces in *Cards on the Table*, but Race appears in a number of novels by himself. Can you recall the name of the Colonel's distant relative who died intestate and so made Race — "a man whom he hardly knew" — the beneficiary of millions in *The Man in the Brown Suit*?

18. Although a confirmed bachelor, Colonel Race in the case above proposed marriage to a young woman. What was the name of the woman who rejected the Colonel's suit, opting instead for *The Man in the Brown Suit*?

19.    Although he is neither a detective nor an Englishman, this financial wizard wanders in and out of the Christie canon, apparently at will. What is the name of that "yellow whale of a fellow" who worked with Poirot, Miss Marple, and Tommy and Tuppence, among others?

20.    The head of the Special Branch in England was perpetually smoking and thus covered "in a layer of cigar ash." Like the character in the above question, with whom he worked, this individual also worked with Poirot and Tommy and Tuppence. Who is he?

21.    Poirot most often worked with Inspector Japp; however, he teamed up with this other Scotland Yarder in *Mrs. McGinty's Dead, Hallowe'en Party* and *Elephants Can Remember.* Can you remember his name?

22.    Mr. Harley Quin's well-known associate also worked with Poirot on a pair of cases. Can you name either one?

23.    What was the name of the book written by Mr. Quin's associate?

24.    What was the name of the former policeman from the Mayang Straits who functioned as the protagonist in *Easy to Kill*?

25. Although connected with Scotland Yard in an unofficial manner, this man was both the narrator as well as the erstwhile detective investigating the activities at *Crooked House.* Name him.

26. Though Ariadne Oliver is a character in *The Pale Horse* and comes up with a crucial clue, she is not the narrator. Who details for us the events that transpired around that converted English pub?

27. What was the name of the Scotland Yard inspector who oversaw the investigation into Captain Trevelyan's murder in *The Sittaford Mystery*? Hint: His last name was the same as the boatman's in *And Then There Were None.*

28. In that same case we met a determined young woman who hoped to clear her fiancé of the suspicion of murder by solving *The Sittaford Mystery.* To that end she enlisted the aid of Charles Enderby, a reporter with the *Daily Wire.* Who was this heroine?

29. What was the rather appropriate nickname given to Lady Eileen Brent, who figured in both *The Secret of Chimneys* and *The Seven Dials Mystery*?

30. Speaking of that mysterious group, who had founded the Seven Dials and served as the enigmatic Number 7?

31.   Although Miss Marple's help was usually welcomed by the official police, there were those who resented it. What was the name of the local inspector in Much Benham who was "rude and overbearing in the extreme" and who was bested by Miss Marple in *Murder at the Vicarage* and *The Body in the Library,* among others?

32.   What were the names of the two amateur detectives who made their debuts and took their curtain calls in *Why Didn't They Ask Evans?*

33.   Which other Christie creation — also a sleuth of sorts — did Poirot encounter during his trip up river in *Death on the Nile?*

34.   Can you recall the name of the young gentleman who teamed up with Superintendent Battle to ferret out *The Secret of Chimneys?* Unfortunately, this character also appeared in but a single work.

35.   Which of Dame Agatha's creations is more than once referred to as "an advocate for the dead"?

36.   Which stolid sleuth has as one of his maxims: "Never display emotion"?

37.   Which Christie creation uses the personal motto, "I come and I go"?

# Answers

1.  Mr. Quin is always bumping into Mr. Satterthwaite.

2.  The Bells and Motley

3.  Naomi Carlton-Smith sketched Quin, while Frank Bristow apparently used him as a model in his painting *The Dead Harlequin*.

4.  Mr. Quin is quite fond of *Pagliacci*.

5.  Parker Pyne worked for thirty-five years compiling statistics in a government office.

6.  17 Richmond Street

7.  Pyne advertises in the Agony Column of the *Times*.

8.     Five

9.     Miss Lemon, who obviously used her references from Pyne to secure a position with the internationally renowned Hercule Poirot

10.    Pyne employed Claude Luttrell, Madeleine di Sara, Dr. Constantine and, of course, Ariadne Oliver.

11.    Pyne was using the name Mr. Thompson while Demetrius the Black Browed was pretending to be Pyne.

12.    Christopher

13.    Five

14.    Sylvia

15.    Inspector James Leach

16.    *The Secret of Chimneys, The Seven Dials Mystery, Cards on the Table, Murder Is Easy* and *Towards Zero*

17.    Sir Laurence Eardsley

18.    Anne Beddingfield

19.    Mr. Robinson

20.    Colonel Pikeaway

21.    Superintendent Bert Spence

22. Mr. Satterthwaite worked with Poirot in *Murder in Three Acts* and "Dead Man's Mirror" from *Murder in the Mews.*

23. Mr. Satterthwaite authored *Homes of My Friends.*

24. Luke Fitzwilliam

25. Charles Hayward

26. Mark Easterbrook

27. Inspector Narracott

28. Emily Trefusis

29. She was called "Bundle."

30. None other than Superintendent Battle himself

31. Inspector Slack

32. Bobby Jones and Lady Frances "Frankie" Derwent

33. Colonel Johnny Race was Poirot's companion on that tragic voyage through Egypt.

34. Anthony Cade

35. *The Mysterious Mr. Quin*

36. Superintendent Battle

37. Mr. Harley Quin

# Smoking Guns and Other Clues

# Smoking Guns
# and Other Clues

1.    Which book did Hercule Poirot consult in order to help him decipher the meaning of one of the two clues presented to him in "The Double Clue," in *Double Sin*?

2.    In which case did the double meaning of *Paris* provide Poirot with just the hint he needed to catch a cold-blooded killer?

3.    What color was Mrs. Inglethorp's dispatch in *The Mysterious Affair at Styles*, Poirot's first case?

4.    As a matter of course Poirot looked upon legwork with scorn; however, he was rather proud of finding a clue in the case of *Murder on the Links*. Everyone else had overlooked it because it was "four feet long rather than four centimeters." What was the object about which Poirot discerned the true implications?

5.   In which case did a cut-up tennis net and a foot injury that refused to heal lead Miss Marple to the correct conclusion about a murderer?

6.   Can you recall the name of the ship that played such a pivotal role in *The Man with the Brown Suit*?

7.   A bottle thrown from a window, a bath which no one admitted taking, and a pair of scissors all puzzled Poirot until he viewed them from the proper angle. In which case were such disparate elements all vitally important to the solution?

8.   Which case was solved because Poirot realized that a number of love letters never once contained the beloved's *nick*name?

9.   What tasty clue was found in the bushes outside Yewtree Lodge, which was the home of the Fortescues and the setting for *A Pocket Full of Rye*?

10.  Can you recall either of the literary clues that Poirot left as hints for Hastings in *Curtain*, their last case?

11.  Can you recall the case in which an empty nailpolish bottle, a missing velvet stole, and the fact that Poirot drank wine with dinner all figure in the solution of a murder most foul?

12. In *13 at Dinner* Poirot found an object in Carlotta Adams's handbag that did not belong to the dead woman. What did our ever-observant sleuth discover which provided him with a much-needed bit of insight?

13. In *The Secret of Chimneys* a card of buttons, a piece of paper covered with *E's,* and a bit of knitting all proved to be crucial clues. How should they have been interpreted?

14. In *Postern of Fate* Tuppence found a series of underlined letters that spelled out the sentence: "Mary Jordan did not die naturaly" [sic]. Which Robert Louis Stevenson novel contained that fateful clue?

15. Speaking of great authors, what Dickensian-type clue did Henry Carmichael leave with Victoria Jones in *They Came to Bagdad*?

16. One of the major clues involving the death of Colonel Lucius Protheroe in *Murder at the Vicarage* was a clock in the vicar's study that ran fifteen minutes fast. Can you recall the time at which the clock had stopped?

17. Just prior to her murder Mrs. McGinty made an unusual — at least for her — purchase. When Poirot learned what she had bought, it provided him with a rather colorful clue. What had Mrs. McGinty purchased?

18. In which case did the significance of the secretary's broken shoe escape the police but not the ever-vigilant little Belgian?

19. At what time was Captain Trevelyan murdered in Hazelmoor, his rented cottage, in *The Sittaford Mystery*?

20. What silky clue did Poirot discover at the site of each of the *ABC* killings, which enabled him to run them all together?

21. In "Tape Measure Murder" Constable Palk actually wore the key to the murder right into Jane Marple's parlor. What piece of evidence did the policeman inadvertently affix to the front of his tunic?

22. In *The Seven Dials Mystery*, what clue did Superintendent Battle discover in the fireplace of Wyvern Abbey which later led him *right* to the criminal?

23. Can you remember either of the items discovered in the dead Simeon Lee's room that later provided Poirot with the keys to the case in *Hercule Poirot's Christmas*?

24. In one case both Ariadne Oliver and Hercule Poirot were presented with the exact same clue in the form of loose numbers on an apartment door. As you might expect, Poirot realized the significance of the dangling digits while Mrs. Oliver missed their importance. Can you recall the case that hinged on numbers falling off a door?

25. Poirot was finally able to arrive at the truth of the *Murder on the Orient Express* because of the manner in which the victim was killed. Exactly how did Ratchett die?

26.  An accidental remark about what object of furniture provided Miss Marple with a much-needed clue in *A Murder Is Announced*? What was the object in question which shed some light on the problem?

27.  What had been added to the picture "House by a Canal" in *By the Pricking of My Thumbs*?

28.  A blue cigarette case with the initial *K* on it proved a troublesome clue in the case of *The Blue Train*. Whose was it?

29.  Nick Buckley normally did not wear dresses of a certain color, but on the night her cousin was killed, they were both wearing dresses of the same shade. What was that unfortunate tint?

30.  What two items did Hercule Poirot learn had been found next to the railroad tracks, both of which convinced him that his theory about "The Missing Schoolgirl," Winnie King, was correct?

31.  The position of a chair proved of vital importance, for from its location in the room Poirot deduced that it had been moved to conceal an item on a table. In what case was the arrangement of the furniture so critical?

32.  On two separate occasions Poirot saved himself and Hastings from possible death at the hands of the deadly No. 4 because he observed the individual engaging in an unconscious habit. What was No. 4's telltale action?

33. In *Sleeping Murder,* what play was Gwenda Reed watching when she suddenly screamed and bolted from the theater because of the unpleasant memories that had been evoked by the line, "Cover her face; mine eyes dazzle; she died young"?

34. In which of the little Belgian's various investigations did a cut-up rucksack, missing lightbulbs, a pseudo-kleptomaniac and matricide all combine to pose a problem requiring more than one of Poirot's famous "little ideas"?

35. What number figures prominently throughout Tommy and Tuppence's adventures in *Partners in Crime*?

36. Who brought Miss Marple the wrong type of stone for a Japanese rock garden and thus set her on the right track in *Murder at the Vicarage*?

37. What item was removed from the boathouse in *Dead Man's Folly* because even though it was only a clue for the Murder Hunt, the killer, according to Poirot, felt, "It might have given someone ideas"?

38. In which case did Poirot arrive at the identity of the murderer by examining a number of bridge scores?

39. The fact that a dog suddenly turned on its mistress caused Poirot to "think furiously," which in turn led to the solution of the problem at hand. In which case did the canine clue prove crucial?

40.     In which of Miss Marple's cases did a red
        and black pullover as well as the unchecked
        growth of *polygonum baldschuanicum* figure
        prominently?

41.     Bellini's *Laughing Madonna* was an important
        clue in a tragedy in which Miss Marple involved
        herself. Couple the picture with a chance
        remark about German measles and you should
        be able to come up with the case in question.

42.     What objects did Emily Trefusis discover
        wedged up the chimney of the cottage that
        Captain Trevelyan had rented in *The Sittaford
        Mystery*?

43.     In which case did the fact that a woman
        had owned no fewer than four wigs provide
        Poirot with a clue that proved critical to the
        denouement?

44.     One was a plant and one was a true clue. Can
        you name the two items Poirot discovered in
        Marcus Hardman's safe that give the title to
        "The Double Clue" in *Double Sin*?

45.     Poirot once purchased nineteen pairs of the
        finest French hose to help him trap a killer.
        In which case did Poirot use some fancy foot-
        wear to help him run a killer to earth?

46.     The case of Mrs. Boynton's death was com-
        plicated because there was one too many of
        these items floating around. What was the ex-
        tra implement that baffled Poirot in *Appoint-
        ment with Death* — but only for a short while?

47.     What truly physical evidence suggested a clue
        to Miss Marple as she tried to unravel the puz-
        zle of *The Body in the Library*?

48.     In which of Poirot's plethora of cases does the
        following quote from *Macbeth* furnish the lit-
        tle Belgian with a rather suggestive clue: "Yet
        who would have thought the old man to have
        had so much blood in him"?

49.     Which of the *Labors of Hercules* involved a
        missing Rubens, a kidnapped schoolgirl, and
        a hideous painting of Cranchester Bridge?

50.     What did Charles Hayward discover in the
        wash-house, the significance of which, had
        it not escaped him, would have allowed him
        to straighten things out at *Crooked House*
        much sooner than he did?

51.     What role did Tiglath-Pileser play in *A Murder
        Is Announced,* and how did he prove of in-
        valuable assistance to Miss Marple?

52.     What item in the dead man's pocket proved
        to be the catalyst for everything that follow-
        ed in *The Boomerang Clue*?

53.     In which case did a dead wasp and a match-
        box furnish Poirot with some important infor-
        mation that eventually led him to a murderer?

54.     A china jar with a picture of a bulldog on it
        provided Poirot with an essential clue in which
        case?

55.     In which Poirot adventure did a priceless string of pearls, a red-stained handkerchief, and a set of hand-carved rosary beads all figure in the outcome of a case that brought a pair of killers to justice?

56.     Hallowe'en is a holiday with medieval origins. On what *element*al clue did Poirot nearly slip up while conducting his investigation into a murder that occurred at a *Hallowe'en Party*?

57.     In which case did Miss Marple almost fail to see the significance of her companion's glass eye — until it was nearly too late?

58.     What item of clothing proved to be more than just an accessory in Poirot's investigation into *An Overdose of Death*?

59.     Madame Giselle had two of what item in *Death in the Air*? Had she but one, Poirot might never have solved the mystery of her murder.

60.     Poirot once had a case in which he remarked, "Every clue looked *promising* and then petered out and ended in nothing." In which case did Poirot see a woman holding a gun standing over a dying man, only to discover later that the gun that had killed the man was different from the gun the woman was holding?

# Answers

1. *First Steps in Russian*

2. *13 at Dinner* or *Lord Edgware Dies*

3. Purple

4. A piece of lead piping

5. *Sleeping Murder*

6. The *Kilmorden Castle* was the vessel in question.

7. *Evil Under the Sun*

8. *Peril at End House*

9. A pot of marmalade jam

10. Poirot left Hastings copies of *Othello* and *John Ferguson.*

11. *Death on the Nile*

12. A pince-nez

13. They were all *rows* which pointed to the *rose* garden.

14. *The Black Arrow*

15. He gave her his red, knitted scarf.

16. 6:22

17. A bottle of ink

18. *The Clocks*

19. 5:25

20. Stockings

21. A simple, straight pin, which he stuck in his tunic for good luck

22. A left glove with teeth marks in it

23. The items in question were a piece of rubber and a small wooden peg.

24. *Third Girl*

25. He was stabbed twelve times.

26. Dora "Bunny" Bunner made a remark about the lamp in the drawing room of Little Paddocks.

27. A boat named *Waterlily* had been painted in.

28. The case was Major Knighton's.

29. Black

30. He learned that the girl's hat and shoes had been discovered next to the tracks.

31. *The Murder of Roger Ackroyd*

32. No. 4 would use a piece of bread to pick up the crumbs remaining on his plate.

33. *The Duchess of Malfi*

34. *Hickory Dickory Death*

35. Sixteen

36. Laurence Redding

37. A comic book with the message inside, "Look in the hiker's rucksack," was taken away.

38. Appropriately enough, *Cards on the Table*

39. *Elephants Can Remember*

40. *Nemesis*

41. *The Mirror Crack'd*

42.   A pair of winter boots

43.   *Elephants Can Remember*

44.   A man's glove and a cigarette case with the initials A.P.

45.   *Cards on the Table*

46.   A hypodermic syringe

47.   Bitten fingernails on the corpse

48.   *A Holiday for Murder,* or *Hercule Poirot's Christmas*

49.   "The Girdle of Hyppolita," which was also the title of the Rubens painting

50.   He found a chair with "a few fragments of earth" on the seat.

51.   The vicarage cat showed Miss Marple how the lights at Little Paddock could have been killed.

52.   A photograph

53.   *Death in the Air*

54.   *Poirot Loses a Client*

55.   *Death on the Nile*

56.   He nearly missed the "water" clue

57.   *A Caribbean Mystery*

58.     A shoe with a buckle on it — hence the original title, *One, Two, Buckle My Shoe*

59.     There were two coffee spoons on the tray in front of her.

60.     *Murder After Hours*

# A School of
# Red Herrings

# A School of Red Herrings

1.  Red herrings are not always red, but this one certainly was. What colorful "clue" did Poirot discover concealed in his own luggage aboard the Orient Express?

2.  Speaking of plants, what had been hidden under Poirot's seat in *Death in the Air* that seemed to point to the detective as a killer — a fact with which Poirot took no little umbrage?

3.  Can you name the two people who both confessed to murdering Colonel Lucius Protheroe in *Murder at the Vicarage*?

4.  In "Murder in the Mews" a set of golf clubs proved to be the real clue. What did the heroine, Jane Plenderlith, throw into a lake so as to mislead the police?

5. Can you recall the name of the living red herring who was dangled in front of the sleuths in *Murder in Three Acts*?

6. In *The Man in the Brown Suit* almost everyone wanted to stay in one particular cabin aboard the *Kilmorden Castle*; however, they had been misled, for that cabin had no bearing on the case at all. What was the number of the popular stateroom?

7. What *foreign* element did Poirot discover in the bushes outside the Welman home in *Sad Cypress*?

8. One of Christie's most famous "red herrings" may be found in *And Then There Were None*. Can you remember which character fell victim to that fatal fish?

9. On the night she was shot, Maggie Buckley had borrowed an item of her cousin Nick's clothing. As a result, she was apparently killed by mistake. What had the unfortunate Maggie borrowed that brought her into *Peril at End House*?

10. Can you recall the signature on the various letters that each of the "guests" received in *And Then There Were None*?

11. Clocks and watches play key roles in many Christie mysteries. Do you remember what time Samuel Ratchett's watch apparently had stopped working in *Murder on the Orient Express*?

12. Poirot easily discerned a pair of red herrings in "The Third Floor Flat": a handkerchief and a note in the dead woman's pocket. What were the initials on both of these items?

13. What was found floating in the Helmmouth River in *Dead Man's Folly* that helped foster the belief that Lady Stubbs had drowned?

14. Can you recall the bogus name on the business card found in the sitting room at 19 Wilbraham Crescent in *The Clocks*?

15. Although it wasn't the murder weapon, this implement was found close by Lady Tressilian's bashed-in head in *Towards Zero*. What did the police initially believe was the murder weapon in that most unsporting of murders?

16. In which of Poirot's cases did green ink not only serve as a colorful red herring but as an actual clue as well?

17. Under the body of the dead Enoch Arden in *There Is a Tide*, two bright red herrings were discovered. Can you recall the items in question?

18. In *Evil Under the Sun* the little Belgian discovered a blob of candle grease, some fragments of green paper, a pin, and "some burnt animal matter which might have been hair." Whose room was he in when he found these false clues?

19.  Speaking of finding things, Poirot also discovered two items in Roger Ackroyd's summer house. Do you remember what they were and who was responsible for their presence?

20.  One red herring that was actually red may be found in *Death on the Nile*. What had been scrawled in blood above the dead Linnet Ridgeway's bed?

21.  Can you recall the name of the pills introduced into Major Palgrave's room while he was enjoying a Caribbean vacation? They were put there to make his death look less like murder.

22.  What physical disability afflicted young Emlyn Price in *Nemesis* and had absolutely nothing to do with the denouement of that particular puzzle?

23.  While investigating a *Murder on the Orient Express*, Poirot discovered a woman's handkerchief in the dead man's compartment. What was the initial monogrammed onto that little white square?

24.  As long as we're on the subject of initials, in which case was a gold box with the initials "C.A." on it introduced to sidetrack Poirot from the truth?

25.  Here's a real toughie. In that same case, can you recall the name that the woman who picked up the box gave the jeweler?

26.     What name was inscribed in "worn gilt letters" on the small traveling clock that had been introduced into Miss Pebmarsh's sitting room in *The Clocks*?

27.     What color are ABC railway guides?

28.     What "smoking" red herring did Poirot discover in the compartment of the dead Samuel Ratchett on the Orient Express?

29.     In the previous chapter we asked you for the two items Poirot found in Marcus Hardman's safe in "The Double Clue," and we stated that one of them was a plant. If you remembered the items, it should be a snap to recall which was the spurious clue?

30.     What is the biggest blind in *The Clocks,* a red herring so cunning that it stumped even Poirot for a time?

# Answers

1.    While replenishing his supply of cigarettes,
      Poirot discovered the scarlet kimono which
      had been worn by the unknown woman.

2.    A blowpipe

3.    Laurence Redding and Mrs. Protheroe both
      confessed to the murder; they did it to pro-
      tect each other.

4.    A brief case

5.    Mrs. Margaret de Rushbridger

6.    Everyone wanted to stay in cabin 17.

7.    A German matchbox

8.    Dr. Armstrong

9.    A flaming red Chinese shawl

10.   The letters were signed in a variety of ways, such as "Ulick Norman Owen" and "Una Nancy Owen." The point is that the initials coupled with the last name equalled U. N. Owen or Unknown.

11.   Ratchett's watch had stopped at 1:15.

12.   J. F.

13.   A large black Chinese coolie hat

14.   Mr. R. H. Curry

15.   A niblick, which is a type of golf club

16.   *Hickory Dickory Death*

17.   A cigarette lighter with the initials D. H. and a bright red lipstick.

18.   Linda Marshall's fireplace contained those items.

19.   Poirot found a small piece of white cambric which had been ripped from Ursala Bourne's apron; he also spotted a goose quill which Charles Kent had dropped.

20.   The initial *J* had been scrawled in blood — shades of *A Study in Scarlet*.

21. Serenite

22. He was colorblind.

23. *H*

24. *13 at Dinner,* or *Lord Edgware Dies*

25. Constance Ackerly

26. Rosemary

27. ABC guides are not red but yellow.

28. A used pipe cleaner

29. The man's glove

30. Why, the clocks themselves.

# Mysteries sans Sleuths

# Mysteries *sans* Sleuths

1.  Christie's last mystery without a true detective was the thriller *Passenger to Frankfurt.* Can you recall any of the three names used by the globetrotting title character?

2.  In that same book, what was the real name of Franz Joseph, the Young Siegfried, the ostensible bastard son of Adolph Hitler?

3.  Another memorable character in *Passenger to Frankfurt* was the nefarious "Big Charlotte." What was the full name — including both title and maiden name — of this character, who was literally larger than life?

4.  Earlier in her career Christie had composed another thriller titled *Endless Night.* Can you recall the name of the young man who married Ellie Goodman and narrated that particular tale for us?

5.  Ellie Goodman was one of the richest women in the world. What were the true first and last names of the young American heiress?

6.  If you were able to remember that, remembering the name of Ellie's companion and confidante who was fired by her family for deceiving them should be simple.

7.  The tragedy of *Endless Night* was ostensibly caused because a house was erected on gipsy land. What was the name of the architect who designed and constructed the house that stood on Gipsy's Acre?

8.  What was the name of the spiritual individual who held "The Last Seance" in *Double Sin*?

9.  Another of Christie's longer works without a detective protagonist was *Ordeal by Innocence.* Can you recall the rather common way in which Mrs. Argyle was murdered, thus forcing her family to face their test of truth?

10. In *Ordeal by Innocence* the Argyle family, parents excluded, was composed of a number of adopted children. How many tots had the maternal Mrs. Argyle taken into her home, and how many of their names can you recall?

11.    Which of the characters in *So Many Steps to Death,* sometimes titled *Destination Unknown,* do we associate with the number 813471 and the letters BABDG?

12.    What physical attribute was shared by Olive Betterton and Hilary Craven in *So Many Steps to Death,* a spy thriller with enough twists to satisfy even the most demanding mystery buff?

13.    In another espionage thriller, a young woman gets herself mixed up in international intrigue for love's sake. What was the name of the young man whom Victoria Jones impulsively followed to Baghdad in *They Came to Baghdad?*

14.    Although the above book had its beginnings in England, the scene soon shifted to Baghdad. Can you recall who hired the recently fired Victoria Jones and paid for her passage to the title city?

15.    One of Christie's fascinating creations was the enigmatic Mr. Aristides. What did that mysterious man claim to collect in *So Many Steps to Death?*

16.    In that same book, what did Hilary Craven leave behind, à la Hansel and Gretel, so that the authorities could trace her movements across the African desert?

17.    In *Death Comes As the End* Imhotep had three sons. What were their names?

18. Can you also recall the name of Imhotep's only daughter?

19. Perhaps Christie's most famous mystery *sans* sleuth is *And Then There Were None.* What was the last name of the couple who acted as servants of the visitors to the remote island of Mr. U. N. Owen?

20. Each person invited to the island in *And Then There Were None* was a murderer. In a true test of trivia, how many of their victims' names can you recall?

21. Who was the first of the murderers to fall victim to the unknown killer stalking the island in *And Then There Were None?*

22. Under what alias was Willian Henry Blore traveling at the outset of *And Then There Were None?*

23. For a change of pace but keeping our seaside motif, what is the only short story in *The Regatta Mystery and Other Stories* in which we find ourselves not only without a detective, but without a mystery to solve as well?

24. In *Passenger to Frankfurt,* how many circles made up "the Ring," and what were the letters in each circle?

25. In that same novel, what was the name of the secret project developed by Professor Robert Shoreham?

26.  What was the singularly apt nickname of Henry Carmichael in *They Came to Baghdad*?

27.  Just before he died, Carmichael said three things to Victoria Jones. What were Carmichael's last words?

28.  Carmichael died in Victoria Jones's hotel room. What was the name of the hotel in which she was staying while in Baghdad?

29.  Although we asked a few questions about *The Sittaford Mystery* in the "Secondary Sleuths" chapter, there is no real detective functioning in that work; however, there is a spirit. What is the name of the spirit whose message precipitated *Murder at Hazelmoor*?

30.  Which leading role did soprano Paula Nazorkoff select as her "Swan Song" in the short story that appears under that title in *The Golden Ball*?

31.  The first person to die in *Death Comes As the End* was the concubine Nofret. What was the individual's name who died next, in exactly the same manner as Nofret?

32.  What was the full name of the character known as "Glider" in *So Many Steps to Death*? Can you also come up with his rank and his nationality?

33.  Finally, what was Imhotep's profession in *Death Comes As the End*?

# Answers

1.  At various times she used the names Daphne Theodofanous, Mary Ann and the Countess Renata Zerkowski.

2.  Karl Aguileros

3.  Countess Charlotte von Waldsausen *née* Krapp

4.  Mike Rogers

5.  Ellie Goodman was really Fenella Guteman.

6.  Greta Anderson

7.  Rudolf Santonix

8.  Simone

9. She was struck over the head with a poker.

10. The Argyles had adopted five children: Jacko, Michael, Christina, Mary and Hester.

11. Andy Peters

12. Shades of "The Red-Headed League": both women had "a most magnificent head of auburn red hair."

13. Edward Goring

14. Mrs. Hamilton-Clipp

15. Aristides boasted that he collected "brains."

16. Periodically, she would leave behind a pearl from her necklace.

17. Yahmose, Sobek and Ipy

18. Renisenb

19. The servants' name was Rogers.

20. The victims' names were: Louisa Mary Clees, Beatrice Taylor, James Stephen Landon, Cyril Ogilvie Hamilton, twenty-one members of an East African tribe, Arthur Richmond, John and Lucy Combes, Jennifer Brady and Edward Seton.

21. Anthony Marston was the first "little Indian" to die.

22.     Posing as a South African colonel, Blore was
        using the name Davis.

23.     "In a Glass Darkly"

24.     There were five circles in "the Ring"; the letters
        were *A, F, D, J* and *S*.

25.     Shoreham had invented and concealed Proj-
        ect Benvo.

26.     Carmichael was known to his close friends as
        Fakir.

27.     Carmichael uttered the words, "Lucifer, Basrah,
        [and either DeFarge] or LeFarge."

28.     The Hotel Tio

29.     Ida

30.     She sang the role of Tosca.

31.     Satipy was the second person to die in *Death
        Comes As the End.*

32.     "Glider's" real name was Major Boris Andrei
        Pavlov Glydr, and he was a Pole.

33.     Imhotep was a *ka*-priest, or mortuary priest.
        He was entrusted with maintaining the Tomb
        of Meripath.

# Fifty Ways to Kill Your Victims

# Fifty Ways to Kill Your Victims

1.  In *Mrs. McGinty's Dead,* what rather unusual instrument was used to murder the elderly charlady?

2.  The Blue Train was also known as the "Millionaires' Train." When Ruth Kettering got on board, she was carrying a fortune in gems. Unfortunately, she never got off. How was she killed on the Riviera-bound train?

3.  Can you recall the name of the man felled by "Yellow Jasmine" poison in *The Big Four*? He had also authored *The Hidden Hand in China.*

4.  Speaking of poisons, what is the name of the poison made from yew berries which was used to kill Rex Fortescue?

5.      Lavinia Fullerton was the first person to utter the title phrase in *Easy to Kill,* and she soon learned the truth of her words. Can you recall the rather pedestrian manner in which she met her death?

6.      There are any number of ways to poison someone, but slipping something lethal into the victim's cocktail is a Christie staple. Can you remember what Heather Badcock (*The Mirror Crack'd*) and Rosemary Barton (*Remembered Death*) were drinking when they died?

7.      Because Miss Emily French was murdered, it was necessary to have "A Witness for the Prosecution." Exactly what was the weapon used to murder Miss French?

8.      Coshing someone, or beating him to death with whatever's handy, is a most reliable way of sending that person to his just reward. Can you recall the implement used on Patricia Lane in *Hickory Dickory Death*?

9.      Here's a real test. Can you recall the much shorter name by which hy-ethyl-dexyl-barboquindeloryate, the poison used to dispatch Heather Badcock in *The Mirror Crack'd,* was known?

10.    Although unsuccessful, the first attempt on Emily Arundell's life in *Poirot Loses a Client* might have worked with a bit of luck. How was the formidable Miss Arundell nearly killed at the outset of the story?

11. If at first you don't succeed, try, try again, seems to have been the code of many of Christie's killers. What, in fact, was the actual cause of Emily Arundell's untimely demise?

12. Coshing can become an art form with a bit of practice; the variations are endless, leading at times to almost poetic deaths. What was the "weapon" used to strike down Sir James Dwighton in "The Love Detectives" in *Three Blind Mice*?

13. Can you recall the weapon used to murder Linnet Ridgeway's maid, Louise Bourget, in *Death on the Nile*?

14. Sometimes you can trace a poison by its side effects. In *The Pale Horse* people were losing their hair, but that didn't deter the killer. What rare poison was used to do away with Thomasina Tuckerton, Mrs. Davis and Mary Delafontaine in that particular Christie work?

15. Sometimes a killer needs to be quick, and nothing's faster than a speeding bullet. In *Peril at End House* Maggie Buckley was shot three times. The same type of pistol was used to murder Colonel Lucius Protheroe in *Murder at the Vicarage*. For what type of sidearm did Christie's early killers opt?

16. Among others, Mrs. Ferrars in *The Murder of Roger Ackroyd*, Carlotta Adams in *Lord Edgware Dies* and the killer of Roger Ackroyd all died from an overdose of the same toxic agent. What was this dependable drug?

17.     Murders often are staged. In *Murder with Mirrors* Alex Restarick was murdered in a rather theatrical way. What was the means that forced Alex to make his final exit a permanent one?

18.     Which of Christie's popular poisons is perfectly safe when used in the eyes but deadly when ingested?

19.     What was the implement used to strike down Sir Reuben Astwell in "The Under Dog"?

20.     Bob Rawlinson and Prince Ali died together in *Cat Among the Pigeons,* but their deaths were anything but accidental. How was this pair killed?

21.     Can you recall the weapon used to hasten Lady Tressilian's departure into the next world in *Towards Zero?*

22.     The murder weapon in *Murder on the Links* was a dagger that had been custom-made to the specifications of Jack Renauld. What unusual material was used to construct the dagger?

23.     We all know that Socrates died from drinking hemlock. What is the name of the derivative of hemlock that was used to murder Amyas Crale in *Five Little Pigs,* or *Murder in Retrospect?*

24. In Christie's early success *The Murder of Roger Ackroyd,* exactly what type of weapon was used to do away with the title character?

25. In "The Sunningdale Mystery," in *Partners in Crime,* Captain Anthony Sessle was found dead on the seventh tee of the Sunningdale Golf Club. He had been stabbed to death — with what?

26. Can you recall the extraordinary weapon that was used to kill the musically inclined Maybelle Annesley in "The Bird with the Broken Wing," from *The Mysterious Mr. Quin?*

27. One way to commit murder is to get someone in a dentist's chair and then administer an overdose of adrenaline and procaine. Can you recall the unfortunate patient's name in *One, Two, Buckle My Shoe?*

28. In *The Sittaford Mystery* Captain Trevelyan was coshed to death. Can you remember the weapon?

29. Lord Edgware died when he was stabbed at the base of the skull. What rather unexpected instrument was used to inflict the fatal wound?

30. In the case of *The Boomerang Clue* problems began when a man identified as Alan Carstairs was found dead. How was Carstairs forced to leave this world ahead of schedule?

31.  Right up there with coshing is poisoning, and Dame Agatha made excellent use of her days working in a hospital dispensary. What type of poison did she choose for the overbearing Mrs. Boynton in *Appointment with Death*?

32.  In *Death in the Air* Dame Agatha outdid herself. How was the blackmailing Madame Giselle murdered on an airliner — in plain view of all her fellow passengers?

33.  Two unusual murders were committed in *Murder in Mesopotamia*; however, our main interest lies in the manner in which Louise Leidner was killed. Exactly how did the good Mrs. Leidner leave this vale of tears?

34.  From the macabre to the mundane, what was the manner in which Simeon Lee was dispatched in *Hercule Poirot's Christmas*?

35.  What type of poison, one of Christie's favorites, was slipped into Parson Babbington's cocktail, Sir Batholomew Strange's port, and a box of chocolates sent to Mrs. de Rushbridger in *Three Act Tragedy*?

36.  In *Easy to Kill* a number of people died in a variety of ways. Can you recall the manner in which Rivers, Lord Easterfield's chauffeur, met his demise?

37.  Can you recall the equally clever way in which Dr. Humbleby was dispatched in *Easy to Kill*, which sometimes appears under the very apt title *Murder is Easy*?

38. Given the rather *outre* methods of murder described in the preceding questions, the killings that occur in *The Moving Finger* seem almost banal. Both Agnes Woddell and Mrs. Symmington were murdered — if not with finesse, then certainly with élan. How so?

39. Can you recall the name of the solicitor in *Towards Zero* who suffered from a weak heart and died after climbing up several flights of stairs when someone deliberately placed an "Out of Order" sign on his hotel's lift — which, by the way, was working just fine?

40. Of the countless ways to poison someone, certainly none is more diabolical than that which was inflicted on Hugh Chandler in "The Cretan Bull," from *The Labors of Hercules,* for before dying Chandler was first driven slowly insane. How was this fiendish scheme accomplished?

41. What was the name of the man whose head was ostensibly bashed in with a pair of fire tongs in *There is a Tide*?

42. Just as there are innumerable poisons and blunt instruments, so too is there no shortage of objects with which to strangle someone. What was the implement used to murder Mrs. Spenlow in "The Case of the Retired Jeweler," which is better known by another title?

43.    In another "murder" drawn from her dispensary days, Dame Agatha has a man die when eserine, a poison, is substituted for his daily injection of insulin. What was that poor victim's name?

44.    How was Cora Lansquenet done in on the day after her brother Richard's burial — which just goes to prove that *Funerals Are Fatal*?

45.    Can you recall the rather bizarre manner in which Miss Katherine Greenshaw, the owner of "Greenshaw's Folly," was killed?

46.    Ella Zielinsky met her death in a most unexpected manner in *The Mirror Crack'd*. In what way was she given a permanent reminder of her mortality?

47.    Can you recall the decidedly unlucky way in which Lucky Dyson died in *A Caribbean Mystery*? Hint: It was the same fate that Joyce Reynolds suffered while attending a *Hallowe'en Party*.

48.    In *Nemesis* Jane Marple was commissioned to clear a man of murder. While she was going about it, one of her companions died. How was Elizabeth Temple struck down in that novel?

49.    How was Gilmour Wilson, the brilliant young American chess player, permanently checkmated in *The Big Four*?

50.    Can you recollect the manner in which some-
       one tried to do away with Poirot while he was
       investigating Mrs. McGinty's death? Although
       it was an unsuccessful attempt in this instance,
       it was used quite effectively on L. B. Carton
       in *The Man in the Brown Suit.*

51.    Here's a bonus question, because there are
       obviously a great many more than fifty ways
       to kill your victim. How was Poirot "killed"
       while he was looking into the affairs of *The
       Big Four?*

# Answers

1. A sugar cutter, which is sometimes called a sugar hammer.

2. She was strangled with a length of black cord.

3. Mr. Paynter

4. Taxine

5. She was run down by an automobile.

6. Badcock was enjoying a daiquiri, while Mrs. Barton was sipping champagne.

7. A crowbar

8. She was killed by a marble paperweight, in the shape of a lion of Lucerne, which was placed inside a sock.

9. Calmo

10. A thread was stretched across the steps. She tripped and took a nasty fall.

11. Emily Arundell died from phosphorous poisoning.

12. A bronze figure of Venus

13. A scalpel

14. Thallium

15. A Mauser

16. Veronal

17. A counterweight holding up some scenery helped him take his last curtain call.

18. Atropine

19. He was killed with a native club.

20. Someone had sabotaged their plane, and they died in the crash.

21. Lady Tressilian was killed with a ball from a fender iron screwed onto the handle of a tennis racquet.

22. Airplane wire

23. Coniine

24.   Ackroyd was killed with a Tunisian dagger which he himself owned.

25.   A woman's hatpin

26.   She was strangled with a string from her own ukelele.

27.   Mr. Amberiotis

28.   He was beaten to death with a green baize sandberg — the kind that is usually placed at the bottom of a door to keep out drafts.

29.   A corn knife

30.   He was pushed into a chasm, suffered a broken back and died moments later — but not before he asked Bobby Jones, "Why didn't they ask Evans?"

31.   Digitoxin

32.   She was stuck in the neck by a thorn dipped in the venom of a boomslang, or tree snake.

33.   She died from a blow to the head by a heavy quern.

34.   His throat was cut.

35.   Nicotine

36.   He was crushed by a stone pineapple.

37.   An infected dressing was deliberately applied to a wound in his finger.

38.   Mrs. Symmington unwittingly drank cyanide, while Agnes Woddell was knocked out and stabbed at the base of the skull with a sharpened kitchen skewer.

39.   Mr. Treves

40.   The alkaloid of atropine was introduced in his shaving cream and thus slowly ingested over a long period of time.

41.   Charles Trenton, a.k.a. Enoch Arden

42.   She was strangled with a tape measure, hence the story's more popular title "The Tape-Measure Murder."

43.   Aristide Leonides

44.   She was bludgeoned about the head and face with an axe or hatchet.

45.   She was stabbed — not shot — through the throat with an arrow that pierced her jugular vein.

46.   Someone filled the atomizer she used for her hayfever with cyanide.

47.   Their heads were held under water until they drowned.

48. Miss Temple succumbed to injuries sustained when struck by a boulder, which was deliberately rolled down a mountain.

49. He was electrocuted when his white bishop hit a spot on a wired chessboard.

50. Someone tried to push Poirot in front of a train; fortunately, the attempt was unsuccessful. Mr. Carton was not so lucky.

51. A bomb was planted in Poirot's flat, presumably by the dreaded "Destroyer."

# Mise en Scène

# Mise en Scène

1.    Roger Ackroyd has been described as "the most famous victim in detective fiction." If that is true, then his home is the most famous scene of the crime in detective fiction. What is the name of the Ackroyd estate?

2.    What is the name of the island on which we might find the Jolly Roger Hotel, where Poirot was staying when he encountered and dealt with *Evil Under the Sun*?

3.    Tourists are always delighted with the magnificence of English country estates. Which estate, obviously a titled one, is listed as No. 3 in *Historic Homes of England*? Hint: It figures in two different Christie mysteries.

4.  In several adventures *The Mysterious Mr. Quin* and his on-looking accomplice met at a London eatery. What was the name of that little-known yet oft-frequented restaurant?

5.  Speaking of restaurants, what was the name of that well-known London eatery in which Rosemary Barton and a year later her husband, George, were murdered in exactly the same manner? Colonel Race was present for the latter tragedy but unable to prevent it.

6.  Like *Evil Under the Sun, And Then There Were None* is set on an island. Can you recall the name of the bit of land that serves as the backdrop to one of Christie's most famous mysteries?

7.  The ABC murders were all committed in southern England. How many of the towns involved can you name?

8.  Hastings's friends, the Robinsons, got a great deal on a flat in London. What was the number of the infamous "cheap flat," and what was the name of the building in which it was located?

9.  What is the address of the Seven Dials Club in London, and what is the proprietor's name?

10. What was the number of the compartment on the Orient Express occupied by Samuel Edward Ratchett, in which he was killed?

11. Can you recall the feminine names of the homes owned by the Renaulds and the Daubreuils in *Murder on the Links*? And if you remember those, perhaps you can also conjure up the name of the neighboring town?

12. "The Mousetrap" is set in a guest house owned by Molly and Giles Davis. What is the name of that now-famous estate, which can still be seen on stage in London?

13. What was the name of Lady Tressilian's estate, at which she met a most untimely demise in *Towards Zero*?

14. When she wished, Dame Agatha could move out of the drawing room and "murder" someone in a rather unexpected setting, such as in *Death in the Air*, where the murder took place on a plane. What was the name of the aircraft in that case, which boasted Hercule Poirot on its passenger manifest?

15. Although he hated to travel, Poirot quite obviously got around. Can you recall the name of the vessel on which he was traveling when he suddenly encountered *Death on the Nile*?

16. What was the name of Sir Eustace Pedler's estate, in which *The Man in the Brown Suit* ostensibly murdered Mrs. de Castina?

17. As anyone can tell you, a mews is an area of carriage houses and living areas built around a courtyard or street; and as every Christie fan knows, there was once a "Murder in the Mews." Do you remember the name of that particular mews?

18.  One of Poirot's most challenging cases was *The Big Four.* Can you recall the place where Poirot bearded that nefarious quartet in their den?

19.  Which of the Christie mysteries should we associate with the address 7 Cheviot Place?

20.  What was the name of the ancient Angkatell estate, which meant so much to all of the characters in *Murder After Hours*?

21.  We all know that the Bantry family woke one morning to discover *The Body in the Library.* What was the name of their home?

22.  The painter Amyas Crale died while painting Elsa Greer's portrait. What was the location of the *mise en scène* on his estate, Alderbury?

23.  In *The Moving Finger* Jane Marple left her village but still managed to draw those famous parallels between residents of her hamlet and the inhabitants of another town. In which town was *The Moving Finger* finally stilled by Miss Marple?

24.  In which club was Poirot sitting when he heard Major Porter's recitation, which served as the basis of his introduction to *There Is a Tide*?

25.  What was the name of the school for disturbed young men that Miss Marple visited in *Murder with Mirrors*?

26. The title of *Hickory Dickory Death* is partially derived from the fact that the house where almost all the criminal acts occurred was located on Hickory Road. Can you recall the number of the house that served as the backdrop for some very adult crimes?

27. Sunny Point seems a bit of a misnomer for the home where the various members of the Argyle family underwent their *Ordeal by Innocence.* Can you remember the far more apropos name by which the house originally went?

28. Originally a pub, *The Pale Horse* had been converted into a private home. To which village should we have to travel in order to visit *The Pale Horse,* and what were the names of the people who lived there?

29. Can you remember the exact address of the home that served as the scene of the crime for *The Clocks,* a simple case made to look complex?

30. What exactly was the mise en scène for the events that transpired in *Third Girl*?

31. Considering Ariadne Oliver's involvement with the *Hallowe'en Party* case, it seems singularly appropriate that the case should have begun in such an aptly named house. What was the name of the house where the *Hallowe'en Party* was held?

32.  What was the name of the house that originally stood on the site known as Gipsy's Acre in *Endless Night*?

33.  What was the name of the Ravenscroft estate, which was the site of a triple tragedy in *Elephants Can Remember*?

34.  What was the original name of Hillside, which served as the setting for *Sleeping Murder*, Miss Jane Marple's final case?

35.  If you happened to read the Chipping Cleghorn paper on Friday, October 29, you knew that a "murder" had been announced for 6:30 that evening at Little Paddocks. What is the name of the family who owned that inhospitable home?

36.  In *The Big Four* Poirot's flat was the scene of a crime. What was the name of the man who was murdered in the little Belgian's home after he had warned Poirot about the ruthless syndicate?

37.  Can you recall the address of Poirot's dentist, Mr. Morley? It was in his office that the events that made up *An Overdose of Death* had their beginning.

38.  The Fortescue estate in *A Pocket Full of Rye* was named after the plants that grew in abundance around it. What was the name of the home?

39.  *Cat Among the Pigeons* is set in one of England's most exclusive private girls' schools. What was the name of that ill-fated educational institution?

40.  In *Nemesis* Miss Marple stayed with three sisters in a house that had seen better days. What was the appropriate name of that Victorian-era house?

41.  Poirot began and ended his career in England at Styles Court. On his first visit, it was owned by Mrs. Inglethorpe. Who were the owners when he returned many years later, at the close of his career?

# Answers

1.     Ackroyd's home was Fernly Park.

2.     Smugglers' Island

3.     Chimneys owns that distinction.

4.     The Arlecchino

5.     The Luxembourg

6.     Fittingly, it was Indian Island.

7.     Andover, Bexhill-on-Sea, Churston and Doncaster

8.     The Robinsons rented flat #4, on the second floor of Montague Mansions.

9.      The Seven Dials Club, owned by Mr. Mos-
        gorovsky, is located at 14 Hunstanton Street.

10.     Compartment #2

11.     The Renaulds lived in the Villa Geneviève,
        while the Daubreuils resided in the Villa Mar-
        guerite. Both were located in Merlinville-sur-
        Mer, France.

12.     Monkswell Manor provided the backdrop for
        "The Mousetrap."

13.     Gull's Point

14.     Poirot was flying aboard the *Prometheus*.

15.     The *Karnak*

16.     Sir Eustace owned "The Mill House."

17.     Bardsley Garden Mews

18.     Felsenlabyrinth

19.     "The Listerdale Mystery"

20.     Ainswick

21.     Gossington Hall was the Bantry estate.

22.     Crale died in the "Battery Garden."

23.     Lymstock

24.     The Coronation Club

25.     Stonygates

26.     The house in question was number 24, but we'll also accept number 26, since two houses actually had been joined to make one.

27.     The far more sinister name of Sunny Point was Viper's Point.

28.     Located in the village of Much Deeping, the Pale Horse was inhabited by Thyrza Grey, Sybil Stamfordis and Bella, their cook.

29.     19 Wilbraham Crescent

30.     67 Borodene Mansions

31.     Apple Trees, the home of Mrs. Rowena Drake

32.     The Towers

33.     Overcliffe

34.     It had been called St. Catherine's.

35.     The Blacklock family

36.     Mayerling

37.     Mr. Morley had his office at 58 Queen Charlotte Street.

38.     The Fortescue estate was named Yewtree Lodge.

39.     Meadowbank School

40.     The Old Manor House

41.     When Poirot returned to Styles Court many years later, it had been converted into a guest house by the Luttrells.

# A Cross Section
of Christie Characters

# A Cross Section
# of Christie Characters

1.  What was the name of Roger Ackroyd's physician and neighbor?

2.  Speaking of physicians, who was the young medical man who brought Poirot into the Farley "suicide" in "The Dream," and later cared for Norma Restarick in *Third Girl* at the little Belgian's request?

3.  One of the most fascinating characters in the entire Christie canon is a private investigator who specializes in gathering information and who never looks directly at people when he's speaking with them. Can you recall the name of this man, who proved invaluable to Poirot on a number of occasions?

4.     What was the *real* name of the title character in "The Girl in the Train"?

5.     While investigating the *Murder on the Links* Poirot ran up against a "human foxhound" from the Sureté who lost a 500-franc wager to the little Belgian. What was the name of that overly industrious investigator?

6.     Can you recall the common name of the nurse who served as a female Hastings in *Murder in Mesopotamia* and the sheep-like companion to Lady Matilda Checkheaton in *Passenger to Frankfurt*?

7.     Miss Marple's first case was *Murder at the Vicarage*. What are the full names of the vicar and his wife?

8.     In "The Perfect Maid," what was the name of the redoubtable domestic who gave the story its title?

9.     Under what name had Anthony Browne been imprisoned in *Remembered Death*?

10.     What was the name of the well-shod woman who lost the buckle to her shoe in *An Overdose of Death*, or *One, Two, Buckle My Shoe*?

11.     Although he stated frequently that he did "not approve of murder," Hercule Poirot described the crime committed in "The Mystery of the Baghdad Chest" as "a perfect murder." Who was the victim?

12.     Perhaps the most repugnant character in the entire Christie canon was the malevolent Mrs. Boynton. What was this malicious individual's former occupation?

13.     Speaking of the Boyntons, how many people made up the *famille,* and what were their names?

14.     Can you recall the name of the man who fancied himself a modern Mephistopheles, and who "collected" killers who had gotten away with their crimes but paid for his knowledge with his life?

15.     What was the name shared by one of the Argyle daughters who married in *Ordeal by Innocence* and a voluble con-woman who tried to outwit Poirot in "Double Sin"?

16.     What was the name of Louise Leidner's first husband, who had been "executed" as a German spy during World War I, but who may have been alive and party to a *Murder in Mesopotamia?*

17.     What was the real name of the hard but fair Frenchwoman who was better known as Madame Giselle? She earned her living by blackmail until she met her *Death in the Air.*

18.     Most actors take a stage name. Can you recall the real name of that widely acclaimed thespian Sir Charles Cartwright, whose home was the setting for the opening segment of a *Three Act Tragedy?*

19.     Possibly you recall the unusual nickname of Miss Lytton Gore from that same story as being "Egg." Can you remember her true Christian name?

20.     What was the surname of the family whose tragedy led to a *Murder on the Orient Express*?

21.     No one in Chipping Cleghorn really expected anyone to die when they picked up their newspapers and read "*A Murder Is Announced*." Still, someone did die. What was the victim's name?

22.     What was the name of Miss Marple's friend who was a former commissioner of Scotland Yard? Hint: He was also Inspector Dermot Craddock's uncle.

23.     What was the far-from-flattering sobriquet bestowed on George Lomax by friend and foe alike? He appeared in *The Secret of Chimneys* and *The Seven Dials Mystery*.

24.     Speaking of Chimneys, what was the name of the impeccable butler at that fine old home?

25.     Who was reading a *roman policier* aboard *The Blue Train* and so became Poirot's confidante and assistant in that particular mystery?

26.     On three separate occasions Joseph Aarons proved useful to Poirot. How did this unofficial aide earn his livelihood?

27.    What was the alias used by the Countess Vera Rossakoff in *The Big Four*?

28.    And as long as we're on the subject of the Countess, what was the name of her son, who with any luck might have had Poirot for his stepfather?

29.    What was the name of the Sureté's representative who played so crucial a role in laying bare *The Secret of Chimneys*?

30.    Can you recall the unusual first name shared by Nick Buckley and her cousin Maggie in *Peril at End House*?

31.    What colorful alias did Madame Nadina adopt when she booked passage to Africa in *The Man in the Brown Suit*?

32.    Under what name did Anthony Cade travel to England in *The Secret of Chimneys*?

33.    Speaking of that case, what royal sobriquet had been bestowed on the greatest jewel thief of the age?

34.    From the criminal to the divine. What was the name of the absent-minded clergyman who returned to his room *At Bertram's Hotel* only to find himself face to face with his double?

35.    In that same case we learned the paternal nickname of Chief Inspector Davy of Scotland Yard. What is it?

36.     Can you remember the name of the *au pair* girl whose body Poirot discovered when he heard the nursery rhyme, "Ding, dong, dell, pussy's in the well," in *Hallowe'en Party*?

37.     What was the name of the glass-eyed major whose physical impairment provided the insightful Miss Marple with a clue that proved invaluable in unraveling *A Caribbean Mystery*?

38.     With his Sicilian bandit's cape and his penchant for irony at the wrong time, this man was the protagonist of *Passenger to Frankfurt*. Name him.

39.     Mr. Rafiel employed a private secretary, whom Miss Marple first encountered in *A Caribbean Mystery*. While working on *Nemesis* Miss Marple had occasion to look her up again. What was the young woman's name?

40.     Secret agents and marine biologists seem an odd combination; nevertheless, one of Christie's creations practiced both of these professions. What was the character's name?

41.     Tennyson's *Idylls of the King* is mentioned in a number of Christie mysteries. In which of them do we actually find characters bearing the names of those famous knights of the Round Table, and which knightly names did Christie choose for her characters?

42.     What was the name of the injured airman who served as the narrator of *The Moving Finger*? Can you also recall his sister's name?

43. What was the name of the character against whom the "Witness for the Prosecution" was giving testimony?

44. What was the full name of the man initially arrested for *The ABC Murders*?

45. Here's a real toughie. What is the name of the youngest murder victim in the entire Christie canon?

46. Can you recall the name of Poirot's secretary's sister, who was responsible for involving the little Belgian in the *Hickory Dickory Death* mystery?

47. Speaking of *Hickory Dickory Death,* who owned the student hostel at which all the trouble occurred?

48. The group on the Orient Express was an odd assortment. What were the names of the two men who "assisted" Poirot with his investigation? One was a *Wagon Lit* director, and the other was a Greek physician.

49. *Cat Among the Pigeons* was set in one of England's more fashionable girls' schools. What was the name of the formidable headmistress who had been one of the founders of the school?

50. This philandering physician was found dead near the swimming pool of *The Hollow.* His wife was standing over him with a gun in her hand, but it was later proven that the gun she held was not the murder weapon. Who was he?

51. Can you recall the common last name shared by Marina Gregg's physician in *The Mirror Crack'd* and Cora Lansquenet's live-in companion in *Funerals Are Fatal*?

52. What was the name of the family for whom Lucy Eylesbarrow went to work while trying to locate *What Mrs. McGillicuddy Saw*?

53. Like "Bundle" Brent, the vicar's wife in Chipping Cleghorn, who just happens to be Miss Marple's favorite godchild, has a rather apt nickname. Can you recall both her proper name and her nickname?

54. What was the real name of the man who was traveling on the Orient Express under the name Samuel Edward Ratchett?

55. In three different Christie works an old lady drinking a glass of milk asks, "Is it your poor child, my dear?" What was her name and in which books did she appear?

56. What was the name of Emily Arundell's rather foolish companion who was the sole heiress in *Poirot Loses a Client*?

57. Can you recall the name of the world-renowned adventuress whom Miss Jane Marple encountered when they were staying *At Bertram's Hotel*?

58. Can you recall the name of Derek Kettering's mistress, who was a dancer in Paris as well as a passenger aboard *The Blue Train*?

59.	Inspiration comes in many forms. Can you recall the physician who in casual conversation with Poirot suggested that he emulate his famous namesake, and was thus responsible for Poirot's version of *The Labors of Hercules*?

60.	Finally, Poirot's most demanding case may have been *The Big Four,* which pitted him against an international syndicate of criminals. How many of the names, numbers and nationalities of *The Big Four* can you remember?

# Answers

1.      Dr. James Sheppard

2.      Dr. John Stillingfleet

3.      Mr. Goby

4.      Elizabeth Gaigh

5.      Monsieur Giraud

6.      Both characters were named Amy Leatheran.

7.      Leonard and Griselda Clement

8.      Mary Higgins

9.      Anthony Browne had been in prison under the name of Tony Morelli.

10. Mabelle Sainsbury Seale

11. Major Rich

12. She was a former prison wardress.

13. There were six in the Boynton clan: Mrs. Boynton, Lennox and Nadine Boynton, Raymond, Carol, and Ginvera, who was called Jinny.

14. Mr. Shaitana, whose moustaches were perhaps the only ones in London that could compete with Poirot's.

15. Mary Durrant was the name shared by both characters.

16. Frederick Bosner

17. Marie Morisot achieved a certain notoriety as Madame Giselle.

18. Charles Mugg

19. Her real name was Hermione.

20. Armstrong

21. Rudi Scherz

22. Sir Henry Clithering

23. He was called "Codders."

24. Tredwell

25. Katherine Grey

26. Aarons was a theatrical agent.

27. The Countess called herself Madame Inez Veroneau, whose initials are the Roman numeral four — IV.

28. The Countess's son was named Niki.

29. Monsieur Lemoine

30. Both were named Magdala.

31. Mrs. Grey

32. Cade traveled to England using the name of his friend, Jim McGrath.

33. King Victor

34. Canon Pennyfather

35. Davy is affectionately referred to as "Father" by his friends at the Yard.

36. Olga Seminoff

37. Major Palgrave

38. Sir Stafford Nye

39. Esther Walters

40. Colin Lamb

41. Lancelot and Percival Fortescue were characters in *A Pocket Full of Rye.*

42. Jerry Burton, who was living with his sister Joanna, was the narrator.

43. Leonard Vole

44. Alexander Bonaparte Cust

45. Leopold Reynolds is the youngest victim. He was killed in *Hallowe'en Party.*

46. Miss Lemon's sister was Mrs. Hubbard.

47. Mrs. Nicoletis

48. Monsieur Bouc was the *Wagon Lit* director, and Dr. Constantine was the Greek physician.

49. Honoria Bulstrode, who was called "The Bull" or "Bully" by her students, was the headmistress of Meadowbank.

50. Dr. John Christow

51. Both shared the surname Gilchrist.

52. Crackenthorpe

53. Diana "Bunch" Harmon

54. Casetti

55. Mrs. Lancaster appeared in *By the Pricking of My Thumbs* and *Sleeping Murder,* and she is spoken about in *The Pale Horse.*

56. Wilhemina "Minnie" Lawson

57. Lady Bess Sedgwick

58. Mirelle

59. Dr. Burton

60. The Big Four was comprised of a Chinaman named Li Chang Yen (No. 1), an American named Abe Ryland (No. 2), a Frenchwoman named Madame Olivier (No. 3), and an Englishman whose real name was Claud Darrell (No. 4).

# Mystery Miscellany

# Mystery Miscellany

1.  In which of her many mysteries did Dame Agatha mention herself by name as a mystery writer, along with such other notables as Dickson Carr and Dorothy Sayers? Incidentally, this is the only time she does this!

2.  What is the strangest thing about the short story "The Strange Case of Sir Andrew Carmichael"?

3.  Which of the many Christie stories boasts a hero named, appropriately enough, James Bond?

4.  In which paper did David Baker place his personal ad requesting a meeting with the *Third Girl,* Norma Restarick? Although Poirot spotted the ad, he was too late to prevent a murder.

5.       On the list that was found among Father Gorman's possessions in *The Pale Horse*, there were a number of names. Exactly how many names were there, and how many can you recall?

6.       Poirot created a fictitious agency in *Funerals Are Fatal* whose initials were UNARCO. What did those letters stand for?

7.       What was the Intelligence code name for the killer who stalked the students and faculty of Meadowbank in *Cat Among the Pigeons*?

8.       Marlene Tucker was murdered in the boathouse in *Dead Man's Folly*. What was the woman's name who was the original victim in the "Murder Hunt"?

9.       Can you recall the name of the character in *So Many Steps to Death* about whom Christie jokingly but truthfully remarked, "And with long graceful steps [she] walked out of the small salon and out of the story"?

10.     What is the full name of the paper in which the residents of Chipping Cleghorn learn that *A Murder is Announced*?

11.     "Rosemary is for remembrance." Can you remember how many people — and their names — were recalling Rosemary Barton in *Remembered Death*?

12.     Can you also remember the rather unusual nicknames which she and her lover had for each other?

13. What was the name and the breed of the dog that Poirot symbolically captured as a representative of "The Nemean Lion" in *The Labors of Hercules*?

14. In that same book Poirot had to deal with a scandal sheet to prevent England's political climate from becoming a modern-day "Augean Stables." What was the name of that rag?

15. What singularly unsuitable nickname did the Countess Vera Rossakoff have for the large hound she called Cerebus in *The Labors of Hercules*?

16. Which letter indicated the male agent and which the female provocateur in *N or M*?

17. Which of Christie's detectives lives by the axiom "Suspect everybody"?

18. What was the title on the record that read the indictments to the various guests on the island in *And Then There Were None*?

19. What was the name of the gem which was really at the heart of *The Secret of Chimneys*?

20. In which case did Colonel Race, Superintendent Battle, Ariadne Oliver, and Hercule Poirot all join forces to uncover a murder?

21. How many of the victims' names can you recall from *The ABC Murders*?

22. What were the names of the three acts in *Murder in Three Acts*?

23. In *Murder at the Vicarage* there was a light-fingered clergyman who stole Mrs. Price-Ridley's 100-pound note. What was the name of that pilfering parson?

24. Mrs. Hamilton Betts owned a rather unusually colored jewel that was stolen. Tommy and Tuppence subsequently recovered it. What type of precious stone had been stolen, and what color was it?

25. Oddly enough Katherine Grey, Poirot's assistant in *The Mystery of the Blue Train,* and Miss Jane Marple never met — as far as we know — yet they should have. Why?

26. George (or Georges) was the name of Poirot's impeccable butler. For whom did he work just prior to the little Belgian?

27. What was the name of the newspaper which encouraged Anne Beddingfield to pursue *The Man in the Brown Suit* by offering her the prospect of a position should she prove successful?

28. Specifically, what type of bonds were stolen in "The Million Dollar Bond Robbery"?

29. Which American is mentioned most frequently throughout the Christie canon?

30.  What is the proper name for the "ordeal bean," which is the subject of Dr. John Franklin's investigations in *Curtain,* Poirot's final case?

31.  Aside from her own creations, which fictional detective is most often mentioned in the many mysteries of Agatha Christie?

32.  Dame Agatha always tried to keep her books current. Can you name any of the three tales in which she refers to the Beatles?

33.  In both Poirot's last case, *Curtain,* and Miss Jane Marple's finale, *Sleeping Murder,* the killer is referred to in exactly the same way. What appellation was shared by the two un-related assailants?

34.  Which infamous English criminal comes in for the lion's share of references by Dame Agatha throughout her works?

35.  Which book would you read if you wanted to find out the solution to the *Murder on the Orient Express* if you didn't — though God only knows why — want to read that one?

36.  What was the name of the informal band formed by Franklin Clarke in *The ABC Murders*?

37.  What is the most common sport mentioned in the Christie canon?

38. Name the largest of the rubies worn by Catherine the Great and owned by Rufus Van Aldin in *The Mystery of the Blue Train.*

39. Exactly what is "Delicious Death," and in which story does it play a significant, albeit minor, role?

40. Christie makes an almost innumerable number of references to Shakespeare throughout her books. Which of the Bard's works would seem to be her favorite, given the number of times she alludes to it or refers to it directly?

41. What is the only European city that is mentioned in a Christie title?

42. In spite of creating more than two thousand characters, Agatha Christie used the same surname for different characters only twelve times. Can you name either of the two most common last names in the canon?

43. When Mrs. McGillicuddy boarded the *4:50 from Paddington,* what was her ultimate destination?

44. A painting figures prominently in the denouement of *Funerals Are Fatal.* What was the subject of that particular piece of art?

45. How many of the five cases can you recall that were presented by Poirot to Hastings as evidence against the unknown killer in *Curtain*?

46. Can you name the Christie character whose last words were "Alfred . . . Alfred . . ."?

47. Which Christie character died holding a small piece of a thousand-franc note in her hand?

48. Can you name the three people who made up the "Triangle at Rhodes"?

49. What were the first words that Agatha Christie ever had Hercule Poirot utter?

50. Finally, the ultimate Agatha Christie trivia question. If you can answer this, you have the author's sincere admiration. Who or what was Cholmondeley-Majoribanks?

# Answers

1.  Dame Agatha mentions herself by name in *The Body in the Library*.

2.  The title character is never called Andrew but is referred to throughout the story as Arthur.

3.  "The Rajah's Emerald," in *The Listerdale Mystery* and *The Golden Ball*

4.  The ad was placed in the *Morning Chronicle*.

5.  There were nine names on the list: Ormerod, Sandford, Parkinson, Hesketh-Dubois, Shaw, Harmandsworth, Tuckerton, Corrigan and Delafontaine. The last two were followed by question marks.

6.      United Nations Aid for Refugee Centres Old Age

7.      "Angelica"

8.      Mrs. Peggy Legge was to have been the original body in the boathouse.

9.      Mademoiselle Maricot owns that dubious distinction.

10.     That particular bit of news appeared in the personal column of the *North Benham News and Chipping Cleghorn Gazette.*

11.     There were six people thinking about Rosemary Barton. They were: Iris Marle, Ruth Lessing, Anthony Browne, Stephen Farraday, Alexandra Farraday and George Barton.

12.     Rosemary was the Ethiopian or Black Beauty, while he was called Leopard.

13.     Augustus was a Pekinese.

14.     That muckraking tabloid was the *X-Ray News.*

15.     She called the mastiff her little "Dou-dou."

16.     *N* was the designation for the male and *M* for the female.

17.     Who else? Poirot!

18.     Appropriately enough, it was "Swan Song."

19.   The Kohinoor

20.   *Cards on the Table*

21.   The victims' names were Ascher, Barnard and Clarke. An attempt was also made on the life of one George Earlsfield.

22.   Act I was "Suspicion," Act II was "Certainty" and Act III was "Discovery."

23.   Mr. Hawes

24.   Mrs. Betts was the proud owner of a "Pink Pearl."

25.   Both Miss Grey and Miss Marple were residents of St. Mary Mead.

26.   Before Poirot, Georges had been in the service of Lord Edward Frampton.

27.   The *Daily Budget*

28.   Liberty bonds

29.   Lizzie Borden owns that dubious distinction.

30.   The ordeal bean is more properly known as the Calabar bean.

31.   Elementary, dear reader! It's Sherlock Holmes!

32.   The Beatles are mentioned in *At Bertram's Hotel*, *Third Girl* and *Passenger to Frankfurt*.

33.    In both cases the killer was referred to as "X."

34.    Crippen

35.    The astute reader might spot the solution to *Murder on the Orient Express* if he read *Cards on the Table* carefully.

36.    The Special Legion

37.    Golf

38.    The Heart of Fire

39.    Delicious Death is a very rich chocolate cake, and it figures in *A Murder Is Announced.*

40.    Without a doubt, Christie's favorite Shakespearean play, based on the number of references, is *Macbeth.*

41.    *Frankfurt* — and if you got this wrong, all I can say is "Ma foi!"

42.    Johnson and Jones are each used for twelve characters.

43.    She was headed for the home of Miss Jane Marple in St. Mary Mead.

44.    It was a painting of Polflexan Harbor.

45.    Poirot mentioned the Etherington, Sharples, Riggs, Bradley and Litchfield cases.

46. Emily Agnes Inglethorp in *The Mysterious Affair at Styles*

47. Marie Bourget, Linnet Ridgeway Doyle's maid

48. Commander and Valentine Chantrey and Douglas Gold

49. Hercule's first spoken words were *"Mon ami, Hastings!"* — what else?

50. Cholmondeley-Majoribanks was an injured squirrel nursed by Edward Angkatell and Midge Hardcastle when they were children. It is mentioned in *The Hollow*.